'Each time a woman stands up for herself,
without knowing it possibly, without claiming it,
she stands up for all women.'

—Maya Angelou

ACKNOWLEDGEMENT TO COUNTRY

With utmost respect, I acknowledge the traditional custodians of the land I live and write on, the Wurundjeri people of the Kulin nation. I recognise their enduring connection to this land and their unceded cultural heritage. This understanding continues to influence the stories within these pages.

A WORD ON LANGUAGE

I am mindful not to reinforce stereotypes when referring to women in this book.

In my use of the term 'women', I am referring to the inclusion of diverse experiences, as I appreciate that we exist on a continuum of identities.

In my utmost endeavour not to succumb to the binary, I am constrained by the limitations of language.

CONTENTS

PROLOGUE

I am fuelled to write this memoir by my desire to document the journey of women towards freedom and self-expression. It is in the cracks of vulnerability that we find our strength, and through our shared stories that we push the boundaries of societal norms. I hope that, in these pages, some will find a call to break free from the chains of conformity and step into their own authentic power.

Before I delve deeper, there is a memory that lingers: a snapshot that illustrates a moment in time when I understood the meaning of giving a voice to others.

❈ ❈ ❈

One ordinary evening, we were setting up and preparing to open our popular Moroccan Soup Bar: an unpretentious, eclectic restaurant with a bohemian feel and the energy of a bustling market. A place where not only delicious Moroccan vegetarian food was served, but where community, diversity, engagement, and social justice values thrived. The aroma of caramelised buttered nuts, fresh coriander, and garlic filled the air.

As the clock approached 6pm, a line of people began to form outside our door, snaking around the corner. Each day reaffirmed our vision, each visitor a testament to our reputation. Each night brought in a mix of people, representing the diverse fabric of our society. They came from all over Melbourne, as well as visitors from around the world, bound together by the shared desire for good food and a sense of belonging.

The aromas of our in-house, freshly made vegetarian Moroccan food wafted from the kitchen, evoking memories of the bustling souks of my childhood. The walls were painted a rich tangerine and adorned with select antiques, artworks, and photographs showcasing our rich history of hospitality, generosity, and community.

When the clock struck 6pm, the door swung open and the crowd outside surged forward, eager to claim their spot in our lively diner. Conversations filled the air, laughter mingling with the clinking of spoons and the sound of background music. Customers from all walks of life took their seats, each person finding comfort and connection amidst the vibrant ambiance.

Near the entrance, a young couple sat huddled together, investigating a stack of flyers promoting local events. In the corner, a book club group gathered, their conversations animated with the stories they were reading. They traded perspectives, wisdom, and gentle banter. Amidst the hustle and bustle, I glided through the diner, feeling a deep sense of pride and contentment. I greeted familiar faces with warm hugs and checked on each table, ensuring every patron was seen and attended to.

It was 2017. The country was debating the Same-Sex Marriage vote. It had been put to the public's plebiscite, disguised as an opportunity for people to express their views, when all it really achieved was to enable cruel commentary and judgment from the ill-informed about the lives and welfare of a community they had little to do with. What a bizarre version of democracy it is when a privileged social group is invited to cast judgment onto those who are already marginalised and subjected to exclusion. There was nothing equal or respectful about the process.

LGBTQI+ people felt the intensity of public scrutiny and judgment. Many of the communities who frequented the Moroccan Soup Bar—communities I have witnessed grow—would come in for dinner frustrated, angry, or saddened by the situation unfolding.

That evening, a young woman walked in, distraught,

unable to hold back tears after seeing a sign in the sky saying, 'VOTE NO'. She was inconsolable, struggling to understand the level of hatred towards her, expressed by people she didn't even know.

I suppose I could have remained silent and simply offered her comfort, but her distress compelled me to act. Marriage equality was a defining moment for Australia, as an expression of who we were and who we aspired to be. It required us to take a stand. Our silence would have simply made us complicit. I offered her a comforting hug, turned down the music, grabbed a spoon, and 'tapped a glass' to gain everyone's attention. I found myself suddenly very nervous. This was the first time at the Moroccan Soup Bar that I had spoken out to a crowd over dinner in this way.

I proceeded with, 'Good evening. How many of you have eaten with us before?'

Half the room raised their hands and the other half appeared confused and curious.

I was filled with trepidation. I continued, 'Our Government has decided to enable a terrible process— one which has legitimised the vilification of a group of people requiring empathy and compassion. Not judgment. This plebiscite is not the business of anyone other than those who identify as LGBTQI+. I urge you to consider the personal cost and impact on these people. They are our siblings, our friends, our families, our colleagues. No matter your opinions, this vote is simply about affirming people's right to dignity. You may not agree with it, and you may think "No", and that is your entitlement. However, you need to vote "Yes" if you believe everyone deserves to live with respect.'

Suddenly, a woman interrupted.

'Excuse me!' she yelled from her table. 'This is totally inappropriate, especially at a restaurant over dinner.'

For a moment I froze. Then I summoned all the confidence I had left inside me, and in an attempt to reply, to say something, I answered, 'Madam, you have clearly not dined with us before?' Gaining traction, I continued, 'At the Moroccan Soup Bar, you pay for the conversation. The food is in fact free.' I concluded, 'Welcome to the Moroccan Soup Bar. I hope we all continue to have an appetite for a better world.'

The room erupted with applause. Two rainbow kids came up to me and said they felt like this was like their home. It was one of the most affirming moments in the history of the Moroccan Soup Bar. A community embraced us further by accepting a public expression of our vision.

These 'tapping the glass' moments became more frequent. A selection of them have been sprinkled throughout the book.

◈ ◈ ◈

As you can probably tell by now, I am a little unconventional. Most kids are born to ask why things are the way they are. I must have been dropped on my head—born to ask, *Why are things not better than this*? Everything I heard in response sounded like excuses, even to a four-year-old—unfounded by any logic. It was always 'God said' or 'girls just can't' or 'in our culture' … I learnt very quickly to seek out God, our culture, or anyone else responsible for my lot in life and for the denial of my expression.

Little did 'my culture' realise, they were only creating fertile ground for me to develop my heightened sense of resistance—and my determination to question and reject the unacceptable explanations of oppressive conventions.

THE
LITTLE VOICE

EARLY LIFE

I was born of migrant parents in the 1960s. Though my birthplace is Melbourne, Australia, my family moved back to Lebanon when I was very young, and this was where I spent my early developmental years, navigating a world shaped by war.

In her younger years, in 1940s Lebanon, my mother was a natural beauty. She had an innocence about her, admired by many, yet she herself was oblivious to it. She existed in awe of the beauty of many other women, never recognising her own. She was tall, elegant, and possessed a gentle tenderness that became her. Like many Muslim women of her era, her aspirations were devoted to the wellbeing of her children. She possessed a generosity of spirit and kindness. She forged a legacy out of forgiving even the most unforgivable.

My mother married my father at the age of eighteen. He was the cliché: tall, dark, and handsome, and a relative stranger to Lebanon—he was Moroccan. While my mother's family encouraged her to get married, they had reservations about my father, but my mother insisted she was willing to marry. To her family, my father was a foreigner. He was not from Lebanon, an unknown. Still, my parents married, and before long they had children of their own. Two years into their marriage and with two small children to care for, a son and daughter, my father left Lebanon in search of better opportunities and, dare I imagine, a sense of belonging.

He travelled to Australia by boat—many months of journeying across the seas with the promise of establishing a better future.

Communication was not readily available in those days—a world unconnected, where even telephones were a luxury many could not afford. A letter to my mother took months to arrive and could take weeks to find someone who could read it for her.

Finally, a year after his departure, my mother received a letter from my father. He explained he could not return, that things had not gone as planned, and that Australia was a difficult place to raise a family. He was still moving from one job to another. One year led to the next, and the next, and the next. While apart, they grieved the loss of one child when their firstborn, my oldest brother, died at the age of six. (Though it feels odd to even call him my brother, as he passed away before I was born.) This loss heightened my mother's grief—her sense of abandonment—and carved a permanent hole in her heart.

During this period, my mother lived with her family; two brothers and a sister. Civil unrest and war punctuated their lives. She was close to her older brother, who cared for her and her two children while my father was away. He provided them with the basics, including financial and emotional support. He was a kind man. On a seemingly normal day, when he was returning home from work, he was shot on the front steps of his workplace. Another victim of the tensions in Lebanon. To his mother, he was the eldest son. To *my* mother, he filled the void of responsibility my father had left—he had been her provider. This loss crystallised her grief. A grief both women never recovered from.

After fourteen years of being apart, my father finally organised for my mother and my eldest sister (their remaining child) to join him in Australia, where they began their communal life.

My parents lived with my eldest sister and her husband in Melbourne, and in 1964, both my mother and sister gave birth. I was one of these children, becoming a part of a single, extended family unit.

I absolutely loved and adored my mother. I fought anyone who upset her and I defended her shortcomings.

In Melbourne, she found herself in a society and world

she rarely understood, surrounded by a language she had never learnt, and within a culture so far removed from any sense of familiarity. She had another son, as well as more daughters. We were five girls and a boy.

Some days, my mother would just weep inconsolably. I never understood why, as she could never express the reason for her despair. She would call out to her siblings, her loved ones, her own mother, or to Allah. Her wailing would start with a whisper and escalate to a complete crescendo—'Y'a khayety y'a Habibi, y'a mama y'a Allah'— until she worked herself up into a trance-like state. A deep longing that none of us could satiate.

My mother became more and more depressed, and the family decided to move back to Lebanon in the 1970s during my pre-pubescent years. We expected she would be happier there. But instead of being welcomed in by her family, we were, at best, tolerated. I found it hard to engage with a culture so foreign, to belong, and to find connection. I was constantly longing for that sense of family, but with a Moroccan father, we were seen as outsiders. To my young mind, it seemed that in Lebanon, everybody knew everybody else. We were often asked who our family was—information which would ordinarily be gathered from our surname, but most did not recognise ours. Only when we mentioned our mother's maiden name did we get a response: 'Ah, yes,' they would exclaim. A family well-known and respected.

Ironically, my mother's family in Lebanon found us odd—our language unnerving—and treated us more as outsiders. This was not helped by the fact that my father left us again, in Lebanon this time.

With very little financial support, our welfare and wellbeing were at the discretion of my mother's family. Relocating from Australia, we had the means to buy a house, but we could not afford the daily costs of living, nor of feeding our family. It seemed my father had left us to languish in a country in turmoil with a comfortable house but in search of life's basics—food, electricity, protection, and safety connections.

Through necessity, I adapted very quickly. I stepped into the role of men and boys without much difficulty. I became the one they relied on to solve our problems. I developed the skills for basic mechanical work: I fixed pumps, motors, doorhandles—I also learnt to fix emotions, especially when my mother was sad and longing desperately.

My only brother, who is four years older ... well, he was the boy. Through no fault of his own, he was given everything and then some, pampered and celebrated on every occasion. My mother even made special 'foods for boys'—egg yolk, honey and milk, a steak fillet—when the rest of us barely had bread to eat. It was a strange entitlement, given that he would often go to the bakery and come back empty-handed, thereby prompting my mother to send me in the hope that I could somehow wrestle through the crowds and bring home some fresh bread (which I always managed to). At home, we had five hungry mouths to feed, and yet the celebrated boy did not seem to help my mother provide.

❀ ❀ ❀

In Lebanon, cultural norms, social etiquette, and rules differed greatly to those I had known in my very early years in Australia. Men and women existed separately: public spaces were largely reserved for men, whereas private and domestic roles and responsibilities were for women. Women would not go shopping for groceries, would not sit in cafés, and would not work outside of their homes. Moving to Lebanon, our fortunes dramatically changed—the system did not support a single mother caring for five children. We met each day with worry and anticipation about where our next meal would come from or if the schools would open, given the civil unrest. Yet, ironically, some things seemed the same. God followed us to Lebanon—the same god who afforded men and boys many, many liberties and denied women and girls the most basic of entitlements.

During this time, I couldn't help but ask myself, *Why are things this way?* Why are boys so special? Why is there special *food* for boys? Why can't girls go to camp, or join scouts, or be engineers, or fly a plane? My mother would often say, 'Girls cannot eat certain foods, it will make them strange.' I believed her. On one occasion, she even bought my brother a bicycle for his birthday—this, when we were so poor that, at times, we went to bed hungry.

Many times, I wished I were a boy. I wondered what it would be like to be seen, cared for, and considered in every decision our family made. I wished my mother would see me in the same way.

Perhaps if I learnt to ride his bike, she would notice me more. I became determined. The bike was too big, and my feet did not reach the pedals, so I learnt to peddle standing up. I would ride and crash and ride and crash, but I was driven. I grew up with the belief that God only looked after boys, and so I wanted to emulate their image, but all the while, I constantly wondered *why*. I kept a mental note to ask God that question again when I was older.

This was the environment in which I was raised. My older sister had a closer relationship to my younger sister than I had to either of them. They had similar personalities and childhood carry-ons. They got up to the usual mischief that kids do—flirting with boys, sneaking out, coming up with the most creative ways of getting out of the household chores. I envied them. I wished I could exist in that innocence of life, but it all felt so far away from me. The closest I could get to this feeling of trust and security was in protecting my youngest sister. In her I saw myself. I was certain she needed to be cared for. Defended.

❁ ❁ ❁

I've always held the view that if the home has an anatomy, the kitchen is its beating heart, and the women are its soul.

The kitchen has traditionally been a place reserved for

women and girls; where interactions are not guided by the formalities observed in other environments.

From a young age, this was my favourite room. I learnt a lot here and always felt safe. I observed the women who gathered to help my mother with meal preparation, pickling, and preserving for the next season. As though by magic, they produced the most amazing spreads from the simplest of ingredients. Formalities gave way to laughter, gossip, and chatter. Women were happy and seemed free in a way I did not witness elsewhere. In their presence, I learnt much more about life than I ever had through formal education.

In the kitchen, I also witnessed my mother's vulnerability. If I caught her in tears, she would feign that it wasn't sadness that made her cry—rather, it was because she was chopping onions. She told me that placing an onion peel on her head would stop the flow of tears (apparently a local tradition). Believing her, I would peel an onion for her to stop her from crying.

She seemed a lot more at ease in the kitchen— unburdened by expectations or constraints. She showed tenderness and humour, guiding us through meal preparation and passing on rituals. At times, she infused these lessons with playfulness, including displays of her very uncoordinated dance moves.

It was also in the kitchen, amongst friends and aromas, that plots emerged, seeding ideas that would be further formalised in the salon (the lounge room).

Yet, even as a very young child, I felt estranged from

what was expected of me. I never felt the same as my siblings, and I did not fit into my environment. I could never just accept what I was told but instead kept questioning, 'Why?', only to be given the same non-sensical response— 'It's our culture.'

'Our culture' seemed to communicate its desires through my parents, particularly my mother, but remained elusive to me. As I grew older, I was surprised to discover that these cultural 'desires' were subjective and passed down through an oral legacy from mother to daughter. The kitchen was a perfect space to cultivate and nourish culture. Storytelling and traditions became infused with the ingredients of each meal, shaping the roles of women and girls within our families and communities.

I will forever treasure the memories of those moments shared with my mother in this special room. I learnt not just how to cook, but also the importance of women's connection. In this way, I finally discovered the culture my mother always referred to.

This was the very realisation that drew me back to the kitchen, back to the enchantment of food and the aromas of cooking. Cooking and hospitality became my platform to engage with social issues, and for my quest to challenge women's roles and reject the societal norms which propagate inequality. I sought to communicate and create my own tradition, bringing me back to the kitchen, back to food, and back to cooking.

❁ ❁ ❁

The sound of soulful Arabic music often filled our house—
evidence of my mother's yearning for a life she never had.
A life that was unattainable except through the words of
the Egyptian soul singer, Oum Kalthoum, whose lyrics
and melody often combined Arabic traditions of love and
longing with their unattainable *expression*, encapsulating
the reality of unfulfilled desire.

Oum Kalthoum's music is emotionally charged.
Soul-stirring vocals are accompanied by an orchestra of
instruments. The oud, qanun, and ney all evoke nostalgia,
and are coupled with modern instruments like the guitar,
keyboard, bass, and drums, to transport us back to the
here and now. My mother lived her life through the ever-
present themes of love and longing. And so, she always
played Oum Kalthoum, the resonant melodies often
leaving her in a meditative state.

These times were paradoxical. Within our
impoverished existence and social unrest, there were still
rituals which needed to be upheld. The salon was reserved
for formal events and was mostly out of bounds for us.
It was the room we never entered, where white sheets
covered the lounges, rugs were rolled up and put aside,
and tableware was displayed in the vitrine.

Once a month, my mother would host an 'open salon',
an istiqbāl, where she unveiled our house to the welcome
of strangers. I became fond of these occasions. I would

look forward to these gatherings so much that I developed a greater understanding of time—learning they happened every four weeks. The salon came alive with the smoking of arghileh passed from one person to another, impressed by the rich tobacco flavour—they were able to taste the difference between the cheaper brands and the 'ajamy' brand. My mother never smoked arghileh herself, but always had it prepared for her guests.

Preparations always began by removing the crisp, clean white sheets from the lounge setting. Our house had to be immaculate. Sweeping and mopping, I participated with excitement for the coming-together of the women. I was always ready to help, eagerly anticipating the food, the laughter, the theatre. It was a performance, as though I was entering a parallel world. It was also an adult-only affair, which meant I had to think of ways to make myself smaller and try not to be seen. I sat in corners, hoping no one would notice, yet longing for somebody to see me, to comfort me—someone who understood what I was feeling.

At the istiqbāl, the best aspects of our family were on show. My mother presented a wonderful image of our lives. It was the image she wanted other women to see, as was customary for the made-up reality of the salons. The finest of foods and fruits were on offer, when most of the time all we ate was bread, zaatar, and zayt (oregano, sumac, dried herbs and olive oil). Somehow, my mother managed to provide the best for these occasions. We were surely the object of other women's envy. So many women coming together. Our neighbours, mums, cousins, acquaintances, and so many families. It never ceased to amaze me how they all seemed to know each other.

They all dressed to impress one another. Awaiting acknowledgment and approval from the other women. I would scan the room, watching everyone, in search of ... I was never sure what, or who. Nobody saw me.

The women's whispers and secrets would fill the room, the sharing of stories, the onward passing of traditions. The ritual was always the same, transforming our salon into a welcoming space for women to laugh, be entertained, and experience joy. I always wondered if these women had children like me.

The intimacy that defined my formative years was informed by the relationships between women at our salons, sharing secrets, arranging marriages, planning futures and a way forward for their families. For their children. At the same time, there seemed a strange distance embedded in their closeness—a performance, a veiling of the truth and the traumas—shrouded with furnishings, fruit platters, and sweets. The women had a silent agreement not to talk about what they already knew, and to ignore what was right in front of them. When I sat in their company, I was protected by the superficial formalities of a reality they wished to present to each other. I wished the salons would never end. It was in this presence that I felt safe, distracted from everything I had grown to suffer in silence. I learnt it was possible to live in two worlds at once: the one presented, and the one that we endured.

❁ ❁ ❁

It was around this time, between the open salons my mother hosted in Lebanon, that I met Rafa.

I was at the tender age of six or seven in a world governed by norms, expectations, and restrictions. Our meeting was as if by magic. Destiny had woven our souls together; two very different, kindred spirits navigating a culture that desperately sought to control us but could never truly comprehend us. In my mind, Rafa epitomised the spirit of freedom: she refused suffocating familial restrictions. With her, I could allow my imagination to roam free and exist in the realm of possibilities.

Rafa was a few years older than me, and we were both outsiders. She taught me how to finally ride that bike properly—it became our symbol of freedom and rebellion. As neighbours, we saw each other regularly, finding solace and comfort in each other's company.

Her eyes reflected a purity, a lost innocence, both of us trying to make sense of this unfair world of grown-up expectations. In the safety of her presence, I could reclaim the simplicity of childhood, a feeling that had abandoned me until the moment I met her. In her company, I could simply exist in the essence of being a child. A bond, unfamiliar, innocent, and pure. This was my first profound child's love. And yet, I knew I was not supposed to forge any real enduring friendships, for this competed with my family's expectations of me. How could such friendship be discouraged in this way? How could they take away the only sense of hope and joy I felt at that time?

Rafa saw in me her younger self. She embraced me without the need for any words. She understood. She, too, was a girl. She, too, lived in a world that was unequal. She, too, defied expectations. She embodied my confidence— to ride a bike, to question everything, to challenge all that was unfair, to persevere. I found myself in life with no training wheels, crash after crash, until one day I was … living. It was in these moments of 'misfit' behaviour that I could validate and affirm my existence. With Rafa, I was just a happy, fearless, innocent child.

And then the war started.

The war in Lebanon during the 1970s was brutal and traumatic. Even for the adults, oftentimes it was difficult to discern who was at war with whom. There were many political and religious factions within Lebanon, as well as the outside powers which were involved, including Israel, Iran, Syria, and the United States. This made it very difficult to understand who were allies and who were foes. The fighting escalated into a civil war, where the loss of thousands of lives and the displacement of many more lasted for many years and bore a continued legacy of conflict, resentment, and devastation.

As a child, violence, destruction, and death became our daily normal. We lived beneath the warning siren. Unannounced, it would go off, alerting the neighbourhood of imminent danger, attacks from air raids, or bombs. We would listen out for the deafening sirens which gave us a minute's notice to flee to a bunker we could not reach, instead seeking safety in a corner of our house that was not overly exposed. It was underneath a doorway, as I recall—the strongest part of the house and, presumably, the last place to crumble in the event of a bomb attack.

We constantly had to adjust between the routine of everyday life and the trauma of seeing body parts rushed through the streets, as well as the sound of bombs and gunshots, trying to find food, seeking quiet in the noise. Recalling the impacts of war is like scratching at something that, just beneath the surface, betrays a long-lasting fear, panic, and anxiety.

For the adults, living through war is no doubt traumatic and overwhelming. For a child, however, the experience of war has a more profound impact on their sense of safety in the world at large. I would often wonder, was this the reality my mother longed for? Was this what she cried for all the time in Australia?

As the war intensified, my father—still in Australia— sent us tickets to re-join him. We departed Lebanon abruptly, thus leaving behind the world Rafa and I shared. A world that nurtured me in our profound connection. This sudden ending made my heart ache, yearning for her companionship. I kept her memory within me for safekeeping, using it to anchor me in moments of loneliness and uncertainty.

Many years later, I heard Rafa had migrated to Australia, and I searched for her—there remained an unbreakable thread that connected our souls together.

And then, decades of separation later, we found each other again. The ties which had bound us in our youth remained intact as the years dissolved, replaced by memories and emotions that transcended time. It was as though we had never been apart. While the experiences which have shaped us differ, our core has remained unchanged.

Reunited, we now share stories of our lives; the decades apart have done nothing but deepen our friendship with added experience and wisdom. It is a connection of the heart. A symbol of resilience.

LEARNING

I was twelve years old and spoke very little English when we returned to Australia in the mid-1970s. While being at school was a liberating experience of joy and growth for many, for me it became a source of powerlessness and pushed me further into invisibility. Although I sat in a special English class one hour a week, every other subject was taught in English, hindering my prospects of a meaningful academic education. From my arrival and for an entire year, I refused to speak. I discovered the cruelty of racism toward 'Wogs'—those who spoke with accents. Every day after school, I practiced my pronunciation— '*this*' and '*that*' rather than '*zis*' and '*zat*'—so that when I finally spoke a year later, it was without drawing attention to my accent. Many of us were subjected to ridicule, increasing my sense of being on the outer. Embracing silence was my best defence against those who bullied me for being different.

At home, these formative years were spent in a segregated, gendered universe: the traditions and customs travelled with us back to Australia. My father was mainly absent, either away or working long hours.

As the years went by, my mother became increasingly isolated and afraid of venturing out without one of her children (usually me). We were her interpreters at the local supermarket, her doctors when she was unwell—which became more frequent. The more isolated she felt, the more depressed she became, manifesting into physical ailments which required increased visits to medical doctors. It was 1312 steps from our house to the doctors' clinic. I became familiar with each one. Every bump in the road, every turn, every corner. 1312 steps to think of how to translate the next diagnosis from the doctor in a manner that would not increase my mother's anxiety and fear.

This became my training ground. I trained in the art of diplomacy, learning how to cushion the delivery of bad news. I understood the meaning of cholesterol, diabetes, heart disease, blocked arteries, 'nervousness'. I developed a medical vocabulary beyond my young years. I was my mother's teacher, her counsel, until more and more, my mother's world became less and less; home became her only haven and her children her only world.

My siblings and I navigated our youth without much guidance, forbidden from the activities others enjoyed: on hot days, when we asked to go to the beach, the answer was invariably that the beach was not for us, and certainly not for girls. We were told instead to fill a bath and add salt. I did not understand what it was that they feared about the sea.

We found ways to make sense of life back in Australia. We existed in our parents' blind spot, in plain sight. At times we resorted to forging signatures for permission to go on school excursions. In this duality of our upbringing, we, four sisters and a boy, shepherded one another through the often cruel adolescent years of our shared experiences. I felt protective of my sisters. My younger sister, positioned as the middle child, often lingered in the background, overshadowed by the attention given to others. She and our elder sister formed a bond, an alliance in their mischievous ways. Though we lived within an immaculately clean house and were provided our basic survival needs—food was prepared with the love and attention only a chef could provide—our emotional, psychological, developmental care was often overlooked. Surrounded by a family of emotionally absent adults, we sought comfort in each other, navigating a path through the loneliness and challenges of growing up, each with our own story.

Intimacy and identity could only be expressed and developed between women, mainly with sisters. And we saw ourselves and our futures, our hopes, and aspirations, in one another and in the women who would visit. Discussions about sexual and reproductive health were taboo; growing up, I lacked this basic yet essential knowledge.

The cultural and social norms which sought to mould me—to fit me into a narrow, predetermined role—hung heavy in the air, even if they were unspoken. Expectations that denied my spirit, my complexity, and my individuality. The pressure to conform was stifling.

Did I really want to be a boy? Was I so abnormal in my gravitation towards Rafa—towards feelings of safety and protection? When our societies are built upon segregation between the sexes, the lines of intimacy are blurred. As young girls, we are shaped early on and taught not to question, but to accept. To be submissive. How could I reconcile this when I was required to assume many of my father's duties? Particularly emerging from my experiences in Lebanon, where I had learnt to be the young bread winner, the provider, in high-stakes settings?

While my siblings were oblivious to my plight, the tensions I experienced were shaping my personality. I was defiant and inquisitive. The bolder I got, the more stories would conveniently circulate, making examples of others who were 'socially deranged' or different, relaying the brutal methods of taming such difference into conformity. I remember the mocking and ridicule afforded to those who did not conform, the girls who played sport and wore shorts, the boys who were flamboyant or camp. Even though the mockery was not directed at me, I would always take it so personally, as I found these people relatable—in a way, they were me.

This left me feeling even more lost and alone, struggling to find my own voice and forge my own identity.

Trapped by the weight of expectation, the only place to be free was in my own mind.

So, I lived in my imagination, enduring the unimaginable, all while managing the male gaze. Ten years of my life passed this way; anticipating, enduring, washing, and scrubbing. I learnt to protect and hide my true feelings; to live in fear of ridicule and rejection. There, in my mind, I found solace in the realisation that I could be something other than what society expected of me as a girl.

My expression was first and foremost about who I was *not*. In these years, I developed an acute awareness of my environment and intuition became my close companion. It guided me to survive certain complex situations. Self-imposed silence was my way of having control over my environment. Yet amidst the silence there was always a little voice within me that spoke through my actions in moments of defiance, validating my existence. A little girl who would not, *could* not, accept nor entertain expectations which treated us, women and girls, as less.

As I grew older, I learnt to become a misfit. I learnt to give words to my inner voice—a more sophisticated, nuanced voice that became my companion, protector, and guide. I started to speak up, for myself and then for others. I needed things to make sense, furiously seeking explanations to everything I did not understand, continually coming back to that formative question: *Why*? Who makes the rules?

Why are girls and women treated differently from boys and men? I could never settle for less.

Whether it be in Lebanon or in Australia, women's lives are marked by the same subjugation. Perhaps expressed in different languages and through unique cultural rituals, the systems which uphold and maintain women as lesser than men are nonetheless universal. Women everywhere consistently seek legitimacy from men. Our expression and autonomy are limited at every turn. We are always hindered by the unspoken rules of what we are not allowed to be.

❈   ❈   ❈

If nothing else, learning came easy to me. I was one of the lucky ones. I was always immersed in everything I could engage with, and I always wanted to know more.

Learning gave me back to myself. It taught me resilience. It enabled me to imagine a world of possibilities of freedom. In learning, I found my voice and my expression. I also developed a strong desire to be seen. Heard.

In our special English classes, we were made to learn 'Waltzing Matilda' to the tune of a piano accordion. Our teacher modelled repetitive memory-based learning, rather than explanation and understanding. To this day, I do not know the actual words to the song, but I can hum the 'Waltzing Matilda' tune perfectly—*da da da da da, da dadada da, da da da da dada dada* …

Throughout my childhood and adolescent years, I developed my own method for learning; it was through observation and intuition that I gained understanding. This is how I learnt how to drive a car, how to construct a sentence, how to mimic and parrot speaking English without an accent.

I also learnt to perfect the language of silence and secrecy and how to navigate violence and abuse, the impact of which wrapped around me like a cloak of shame and humiliation for many years.

As a teenager, I was shy and reserved. My mind often wandered—I was preoccupied, distracted by the events at home.

Helen, my humanities and drama teacher, noticed me. Despite my withdrawn nature, she must have sensed there was some deeper cause for concern. She invited me to join the drama class of the year above my grade and negotiated with my mother to allow me to join school excursions. Somehow, she knew I would benefit greatly.

Helen also became a catalyst for my love of reading, which has since accompanied my healing, growth, reflection, and escapism in difficult times. Her guidance, recommendations, and unwavering belief in the power of literature transformed my life. I love the beauty of language and its endeavour to capture the complexity and depth of human emotion.

As I reflect, I am reminded of the power of a teacher's influence—planting the seed, shaping not just our immediate experiences but also the trajectory of their students' lives.

Reading sprouted that initial connection with Helen. It became a foundation of my growth and a guide throughout my existence.

Helen's perceptive nature also became a source of comfort and protection, whether it was in her reassuring smile, her kind words, or an open invitation to chat. In her company, I found a space to voice my worries and talk openly about what I was experiencing at home.

Helen provided support in my difficult teenage years, her influence transcending the confines of the classroom: she was instrumental in eventually changing my life for the better. Despite potential pushback from the school system, she relentlessly sought to intervene and rescue me from a life marred by harm and brutality. Her moral compass was uncompromising, even in the face of institutions which chose to ignore the harsh reality of too many girls' experiences.

Though she could not change the outcome, as I was destined to be married off at a young age, Helen maintained contact with me over the years. Ultimately, it was her constant presence and support which gave me the means to break free.

Helen not only changed my life, but she also taught me the difference one person can make. She instilled in me the value of challenging the status quo and tirelessly seeking solutions for those who are most in need. The impact of *her* support now inspires me to support others daily.

MARRIAGE

Arranged marriages are born from traditions in many cultures whereby families of the bride and groom facilitate the selection of their spouse. At times, it can be a wonderful union that brings two people together who might not have met otherwise; a bit like modern dating sites arrange meetings for the modern times. However, like many marriages (arranged or otherwise), when things go wrong, they go *very* wrong; such was the case with my own arranged marriage.

Melbourne, 1980s. The aroma of Arabic cardamom coffee filled the room. On offer, dates and baklava—sweets reserved for special occasions. The focus was on me, in a ritual I had not experienced before. One of many firsts. My mother had paid special attention to every detail that day: what I wore, how I smelled, how I walked. I recall wearing perfume and shaving my legs for the first time. I found the occasion strangely curious, like a family performance piece without a script, and everyone adopting a predetermined character—from setting the scene, to the welcome, to the offering. I was on display for selection—the promise of my future with a stranger. Yet, despite all this excitement, I felt an inner sense of calm.

I met him, the man who would become my husband, for the first time. I was filled with a sense of anticipation at the possibility of finally escaping; relying on my body's learned, robotic responses to guide me through this encounter.

Learning the motions on the go, I was asked to serve them coffee. My hands trembled a little as I walked into the salon with a tray of hot coffee and sweets. An air of expectation that I did not understand filled the room. The etiquette, the ritual, of greeting my future husband and his family, all eyes on me, examining every detail, my movement, commenting on my height, my strength, my nature—they were thoroughly checking their would-be property as I passed around the coffee tray from stranger to stranger. My only companion was my thoughts.

We met a few times, always accompanied by a chaperone. I felt emotionally detached. I did not understand the situation, yet I also found myself overcome by the prospect of being freed. Two weeks later, we received the call. Apparently, he'd said yes.

I was fifteen years old.

❀ ❀ ❀

The wedding was a small ceremony, not really a ceremony in fact, rather a get-together at my parents' home. I was donned in a second-hand wedding dress, strangers congratulating my family.

He drove us to my new home, a small one-bedroom flat. It seemed very odd that my life would begin in this way. I had no idea how to behave, or what to expect.

As we arrived, his mother greeted us at the door with a large bag in hand. 'White sheets,' she whispered, 'you will need to use them later.'

This reminded me of the white sheets my mother had used to protect our formal furniture in Lebanon. I was flooded with an overwhelming sense of familiarity. I set them aside until they were supposedly needed. His mother gave me clear instructions for when and how to use them. She explained that she would visit us the following morning to collect them, and with those sheets, the family's honour.

I found this perplexing—how could their honour be tied to the sheets? If they were so precious, why did she leave them behind? Even now—especially now—it seems bizarre the stories people tell themselves and expect others to believe.

But there I was, in my wedding dress, with a relative stranger with whom I was about to begin my life.

It was December, a warm balmy evening. As we entered

the flat, he loosened his tie and almost fell into the couch, as though relieved the formalities were over. I examined his face closely for what seemed like the first time: his eyes set close together, the darkest brown, a chiselled nose, and his lips almost purple. His skin was quite tanned, his form angular yet muscly. He was years older than me, which made his expression very difficult to read. I stood in front of him, not knowing what I was supposed to do. He motioned for me to sit beside him. I did.

He made small talk for about a minute … then came the question: 'What would you say if I told you the seawater is sweet?'

I thought to myself, *What an odd question.* I was fifteen, married to a man I had just met, sitting next to him on the day of our wedding, and then came this question. I did not understand it, yet knew intuitively that my answer would be life-altering.

'Oh, what?' I said. 'Of course it's not.'

He insisted, 'But if *I tell you* it is sweet?'

I answered, 'We can go and taste it. If it is sweet, I'll tell you it's sweet, and if not, we will both know that it is not—'

Before I'd finished the sentence, I felt the back of his hand land across my face. The burning sensation of pins and needles. It reminded me of the heat and the numbness of when the dentist once pulled out my tooth. Involuntary tears ran down my face. I pulled away from him and crouched in the corner of the room.

He was uncultured. His mannerisms and behaviours were—to the broader society—normal and acceptable, but in that moment, I sensed within him an absence of humanity.

I was meant to learn an important lesson on my wedding night: the only way in this marriage was going to be *his* way. He had no capacity for reasonable communication, conversation, or intimacy. No logic, and certainly no compassion. His violence became the defining feature of the marriage. It was only in this brutal method that he was able to clearly communicate his intentions and expectations of me.

I wished someone had warned me. I wished I had been armed with the know-how and the tools to navigate my new reality. My new life with a violent stranger.

Even more than that, I desperately wished I could get through to him, or that he would just stop and *see me*. I often wondered what he saw when he looked at me; often thought about how I could influence the *way* he interacted with me. Did I need to dress differently? Did I need to speak differently? How did I need to act? How could I know the unknowable? How could I become somebody else—somebody who could pretend the seawater was drinkable?

Books remained a lifeline during this period. I would visit the local library in secret and read everything I could get my hands on, from self-help books to poetry. The silver lining to his illiteracy was that I could further my love for reading without his intrusion into that world. My escapism was also listening to music which was forbidden at home. I would have to wait until he left the house for work before I slipped out to go to town.

I got to know my local shopping strip and would go to the Sussan clothing store, where they played the same songs from Chrissie Hynde and The Pretenders. I learnt the lyrics until they became more familiar than my own thoughts.

I cherished the ability to keep these sacred secrets.

These small acts of defiance had cumulative effects. They helped me build a renewed taste for independence and freedom and gave me the courage to leave him. To take control of my life.

LEAVING

I became consumed with thoughts of escape. I learnt to navigate the dual reality of being his obedient wife and plotting my departure. I learnt the language of my new normal—to allow him to think that his way had become, in fact, the only way we would live. To make him comfortable and entice him into complacency.

Determined to be free from this life of misery, I gathered the information and resources I needed to leave, waiting for the right moment.

I began to read his moods and his body language. How he walked around the house: the pace and sound of his movements could indicate hunger, anger, or a simple need for silence. I fine-tuned my ability to intuit my next opportunity just by listening. 'Teaching me a lesson'—a phrase he used when he hit me—became a habit of his. He developed his own repertoire in violence, ranging from a slap with the back of his hand to housebound imprisonment. Me being me, I always found a way out!

He would lock the doors. I would just *climb out the window*.

At first, my heart raced in fear. What if he found me? What if someone told him? What if I couldn't get back in? But, driven by the prospect of freedom, I discovered that my defiance presented me with far greater opportunities than mere disobedience. Every day, as soon as he left for work, I fled.

The local shopping strip enabled me to meet real people beyond his family and the imprisonment of our four walls. I spent hours studying the faces of strangers, wondering what their lives were like. I became familiar with the latest fashion items, fantasising about things like buying the latest pair of jeans—I would try on different clothes, knowing I could never buy them, let alone be allowed to wear them. The power of imagination sustained in me a sense of hope. Each day, with every outing and every outfit I tried, I returned home with another reality steadily anchoring itself in my realm of possibility. For the time being, I was satisfied.

I dreaded the weekends. He was always home. He would often invite his family for lunch. Generally, the women would examine the cleanliness of the kitchen, open the drawers, the oven, the pantry, casting judgement. An examination they never tired of. To them, this ritual affirmed their superiority, and reinforced their entitlement to my submission; ensuring I was obedient, hospitable, and compliant. Women policing other women and reinforcing social norms. It was probably their way of affirming their own subjugation: if there was no contrast between their norms and mine, then there was no cognitive dissonance between the reality of their existence and the aspirations they'd had to forgo.

Almost always, I failed, resulting in more violence and more restriction over the little freedom I still had. I recall the mental punishment of enduring his sisters imposing themselves on specific days of the week to teach me the 'right' way to clean.

As soon as the weekends were over, I was climbing out the window again.

I became acquainted with many shop assistants: Sharon from Sussan, who worked two days a week, and Jane, who worked three days a week. Jane and I became friends—well, not really friends, but acquaintances. Someone I could chat with when I walked into the store. She knew I would never buy anything, yet every time I went in, she would treat me with the same attention she offered to any new customer. We both knew and both pretended. I wonder where Jane is now.

I also frequented the local department store. There were too many assistants to learn all of their names. I did, however, become familiar with their faces and would say hi to the ones I came to recognise. I became close to Megan at the local milk bar and would often just go in for a chat. She would see my bruises, which I did not hide, and she would always ask if I was okay, even though she knew I was not. Visiting Megan helped me plan my escape. She was the first to speak with me about safe places for women in crisis—women's refuges. It became evident that *he* would never venture into those places, which meant he would never find me. Megan changed my life's trajectory; I also wonder what has become of her.

These routines became my safe spaces. It was there that I learnt how to dress, how to be, how to interact, how to imagine myself. He could lock the doors, but I would jump out the window. He could lock the windows, but I would break the walls. I found a strength in myself that I never knew I had. He could not kill my will to be free.

Then came the first pregnancy. And I could climb out the window no more.

❁ ❁ ❁

I attempted to leave him several times. I would go back home to my parents' house. With every attempt, I was taken back. He would think of ways to further control and intimidate. Rather than trying to befriend me, which would have been a much more effective way of keeping me in line, his modes of control always turned to violence.

Here laid his creativity, and he was good at it.

Yet it was not difficult to outsmart him. He didn't know about the window, he didn't know about the imagined friendships I forged in the shopping malls, and he didn't know about the illicit music I was drawn to hear. These minor freedoms were what made his violence tolerable, and what made my escape inevitable.

His violence and control were designed to make me obey, but it never worked. Yes, it hurt me, but it did not break me. It seemed ironic that he would continue to use these same ineffective methods, even while I was pregnant with our first child. It baffled me that he would not just *ask* what I needed. This pattern of domestic abuse was legitimised by his surroundings, culture, tradition, and society at large.

A number of times I wished he would just be curious about me, see me, be decent. I wished he saw me as more than an object or his property. Was I just the would-be mother of his children? Someone who cooked his meals? Or was I just a problem he had—a person at home who continually defied him? That his insecurity, inadequacy, or frustrations could only be expressed through sheer force and violence also speaks to his incapacity to reflect on his behaviour.

One day, he took a ride to work with one of his friends. He left the car parked outside. The car keys were still on the kitchen bench. That morning, he was in a rage at me for not being able to keep the baby quiet. In his furore, he had destroyed all the fruits and vegetables I had spent hours pickling: bright pink turnips, cucumbers in brine, chillies, lemon, and olives. I had carefully placed every piece, every morsel, in glass jars before filling them with brine and olive oil. And he smashed them over the kitchen tiles.

The juice splashed everywhere, painting the floor and ceiling pink. I have a clear, distinct memory of finding it odd that such a violent act could produce such beautiful art.

I contemplated cleaning up, as was his order, and as was my habit. But instead, on this day, the keys on the counter caught my eye. With fear and excitement, I contemplated an escape.

My mouth was sour and dry with the taste of adrenaline. I did not even have time to consider the consequences of what I was about to do. I strapped my son in his bassinet on the front seat. He looked at me, calm, as if to reassure me. The car moved slowly; I soon got the hang of it: how to turn, to stop, to move forward. I headed out without a map, relying on intuition and muscle memory alone to guide my hands and feet and steer the car. I thought to myself, *Thank goodness I don't need to parallel park.*

I arrived at my mother's home, to her surprise and astonishment, without *him*. I had never learnt to drive and was not allowed to venture out alone.

❋ ❋ ❋

For my parents and my broader community, divorce was not an option at my disposal. My mother calmed me and fed me, as was her answer to all of life's ills. She gave me strategic advice and told me not to provoke him. As became their habit, she and my father returned me. For every subsequent attempt to leave, I would be returned to what was deemed to be my rightful home. This only reaffirmed my resolve to leave.

The fourth time I left, I was eighteen and pregnant with my second child. I found shelter in a women's refuge. The concept was alien—a secret place where women in crisis came together to escape violence, each woman in distress trying to forge a way out. The refuge was an opportunity for me to escape. Yet, I was entering a foreign world, confronted by a different language, culture, food, and atmosphere.

This refuge was tailored for pregnant women, each with our own trauma and our prenatal needs. The support workers' focus was on the tangible things, such as food, clothes, and our antenatal necessities. Hours of support were limited, mainly provided on weekdays with an emergency contact number listed for out-of-hours support. (Ironically, most women's need for support *was* after hours; in the still of the evening, when our thoughts were racing with unanswerable questions, fears, and anxieties.)

As I disappeared to the refuge, I knew my mother would be sick with worry. So, after two days in my room, I phoned her to reassure her that I was safe. She pleaded with me to come back, and promised everything would be okay if I just told her where I was. I would not have to go back to him.

And yet … I did.

Many more times, I fled to Mum's and was always returned.

He assumed the rights to my body, as though I was a mere vessel through which he could produce children. And he wanted at least a dozen—a soccer team, as he used to say. I could never be that person, and eventually I asked the doctors to insert an IUD (following their discrete provision of information about its uses). Of course, this was done without his knowledge.

He kept track of my periods in order to judge when he could use my body and when to reproduce. He began to question why I was still menstruating. Why I had not fallen pregnant yet. He insisted I go to the doctor to check that there was nothing wrong with me. At no stage did he ever consider the problem could lie elsewhere.

It was then that I felt I had no choice but to have the IUD removed. Leaving became even more urgent.

My final attempt to leave was months later after my second son was born, and this time my father drove me back. Upon our arrival, my husband opened the front door to greet us.

My father, frustrated by my husband's continued violence, said, 'This is your *wife*, your *family*, your *children*. You need to find a way to live together amicably and look after them. I will not continue to tolerate this level of humiliation and drama.'

With a look of desperation, I pleaded with him not to leave me there.

My father sighed. 'I have work early, I have to go.' As I tugged at his shirt, he added, 'He won't hurt you anymore.' And he left. He left me there.

In the lounge room, my husband, emboldened by the reinforcement of his might, stated, 'No-one wants you', 'You'd better obey', 'I can do anything to you', 'No-one cares about you.'

In sheer desperation, unable to see a way out, I became more convinced that I needed to put an end to this cruel path my life had taken.

I put the heater on to warm the bedroom. I plugged in our cassette player, placed it on the floor near the bed, and Oum Kalthoum started singing—she had become my companion, as she had been my mother's companion, to a life longing to be free. I wrote my husband a note explaining his cruelty (and chuckled to myself—what was the point, as he could not read?). I put on my comfortable flannelette pyjamas. The rhythm of Oum Kalthoum's music transported me to a place where I imagined I would dance through life, where he would become insignificant.

The bedroom was dimly lit. My husband was sitting in the lounge room. The smell of his cigarette smoke wafted under the doorway, carrying with it his anger and the weight of his expectations; plotting, planning his next steps on how to maintain his control. In my utter aloneness and depleted mind, attempting to leave—ending my life—was the ultimate act of defiance and freedom. I had tried so many times and in so many different ways to escape, and now there seemed no other way out—no escape from the violence and control which consumed me. I walked into the bathroom, I looked in the mirror, nodding to myself, thinking, *You deserve better.*

I emptied a cocktail of medicine into the palm of my hand and, with an eerie sense of calm, swallowed all the tablets.

The moment I took those pills, I felt a rush of warmth spread through my body like a comforting, calm embrace. I walked back to the bedroom to the soothing voice of Oum Kalthoum. I slipped into bed and wrapped myself in the sheets like a cocoon. I remember thinking I would sleep into the next phase of my life, who knows, perhaps meeting God—it was time for some much-needed answers.

But then came the reality, the nausea, and the dizziness. The trembling. My entire body shook uncontrollably. I called out … I was not sure to whom.

I woke up in hospital. The realisation that I was not dead—the sense of dread at the thought of being made to go back—competed with the possibility of a newfound freedom. So many feelings circulated through my drowsy and confused mind. Most noticeable was a determined rush of excitement that maybe, just maybe, he would no longer be in my life. The possibility to live free of control, violence, a life on my own terms, free to *be.* Maybe I could go back to school? Work?

But the kids—*Oh my God, what about the kids? Where are they? Who is looking after them? What will become of us?*

That was indeed a defining moment. The turning point. My parents' expectations of me, combined with the social pressure of their isolated community, meant they had a choice to make: either uphold nonsensical social expectations of women, even at the cost of my life, or allow me *freedom*. This was a reality they could no longer ignore.

That I am still here speaks to the choice they made. And I am so glad!

As I broke free from the control and abuse of the marriage, I found myself at a crossroad. I refused to be anyone's victim. I recognised myself in every story of hope and survival and was inspired by every song of resilience, optimism, and determination.

This was the beginning of my new life. I was nineteen, mother to a toddler and a baby, and I was free.

FREEDOM

Once I left the violent marriage, the father of my children, determined to maintain control and exact revenge, took our young sons to live interstate; adamant that he would keep me from ever seeing them again. I can still recall the visceral pain of that separation. Few emotions can compare.

Such was my life for many years without my two young boys. I was denied the opportunity to see them, watch them, hold them, or be a part of their lives. Those were agonising years that left a hole in my heart, filled with longing in every fibre of my body. Being separated from my children was, at times, a heartache so severe I felt I would split into a million pieces. I spent most nights yearning for their presence, fearing for their wellbeing, and agonising over when I might see them again.

This was life without my boys: days turned to weeks, weeks to months, and months into years. Every morning, particularly of the first year, I woke up to the awful realisation of their absence. I sought solace from my aching reality, remembering the echoes of their little voices, their laughter, their mischievous ways, the warmth of their hugs. I existed in these memories which provided me little comfort.

I navigated legal battles, advocating for my right to see them, pleading my case to anyone who would listen, all to no avail. The system was designed to deem me 'unfit'— after all, I did try to take my own life. There was little to no recognition of the context which enabled this underage marriage and the enduring violence suffered.

The years passed, each one a reminder of the passage of time.

I will be forever grateful for the role my sister played in maintaining a connection with my two boys. The fleeting visits were never planned. They were marked by random surprise. Through her ingenious efforts, she ensured I could see my children the rare times their father brought them to Melbourne. She orchestrated precious reunions, allowing me moments I yearned for: moments of love, of being a mother. Despite the heartbreak of knowing I'd have to leave them once more, as I briefly held my little ones in my arms, all the anxiety and uncertainty of the world disappeared.

This was the most difficult period I have ever had to endure. The daily anguish and despair, the grief and longing, is incomparable to anything else I have ever felt.

❀ ❀ ❀

After being released from hospital, I moved to my parents' house. As a single mother without her children, I was under much more scrutiny than my other siblings, creating a new source of social and cultural anxiety for my parents. As often is the case for many families, the only way to move forward was to ignore and pretend. Luckily for me, this meant school was deemed the most convenient and honourable excuse for my social absence at home and across familiar circles. I was thus allowed to re-enrol in school as a mature-age student, determined to complete my high school education.

As the oldest student in the classroom, I had the familiar feeling of being an outsider. I learnt to replace this sense of alienation with a sense of belonging. I felt confident in the knowledge that I was paving the way for myself and potentially for other women, holding firm in the belief that it was never too late to pursue the life that I wanted. As I looked around the classroom, I felt so privileged. Being a student, in a classroom, transcended age, gender, or cultural background. We were unified in our joint pursuit of knowledge, open-mindedness, and personal growth.

Unfortunately, the teens were not all that generous; yet their teasing fell on deaf ears. I was there to learn, absorbing every word, engaging with every concept, and analysing every sum. The joy of learning ignited a curiosity inside me. With every new idea, I felt more alive. I decided then and there I would never stop learning.

❀ ❀ ❀

To help with paying the household bills, I quickly sought out employment and got a part-time job. With these new routines, the possibilities I had seeded in my imagination now appeared within reach. Each day felt like a gift, more vibrant and alive than I had ever envisaged. The world felt like a playground that I was eager to join, to try all things, and savour this precious new life. Yet, the intensity of missing and longing was ever present, occasionally tampered by the thrill of freedom. I read many books, self-help mainly, which spoke to a healing I so desperately needed.

I had been released from a cage, literally, at last free to explore the wonders of the world around me. This sense of freedom and liberation afforded me the thrill of discovering new places, new people, and new experiences. After four years of being virtually locked in a house, I was finally taking control of my life, proving to myself (and everyone around me) that I was capable.

As I aspired to the impossible—studying, learning new skills, working—a life I had long thought to be out of reach grew closer, filling me with a renewed determination to live. Years went by, I made some friends, learnt some skills, and eventually regained more autonomy from my parents.

❀ ❀ ❀

For my first full-time job, I found work in a factory—definitely nothing fancy, packaging clothes for Target. The workplace politics and dynamics were fraught with competition: you could not pack too fast, or faster than your superiors, however you still had to be fast *enough* for their approval.

I lasted six months. In the tearoom, a newspaper was often left open on the employment section. Seeing a listing for tram conductors, I applied, and to my surprise, I was accepted.

The uniform for tram conductors at this time was gendered. For men, it was long pants for winter and shorts for summer. For women, a thick skirt or women's pants in winter and a green dress in summer. We were governed by strict rules not to alter these uniforms—the only exception being the length of the pants to suit our height.

In summer, the trams packed during peak hour and the heat was sweltering. At the time, trams had no air-conditioning. It was so hot I could feel my outer layer of skin melt away into the person standing next to me. A scorching heat.

I was never comfortable in a dress; I always wore pants. I decided to cut my winter pants to turn them into shorts, just above the knee. This at least made it a little more bearable to be a tram conductor in summer.

One day we were stopped by an inspector. He greeted me with, 'Hey, mate', then realised I was not in fact a man. He cleared his throat, surprised by my appearance—he had not been trained to deal with a situation like this.

'You are out of uniform,' he accused.

'No, I'm not,' I answered.

It turned out I was the first woman conductor to challenge him by wearing *shorts* on the tram. This encounter turned into an incident, going all the way up to the depot union. My shorts became a test case predicated upon one central question, put to a vote by a union rep: Should women be allowed to wear shorts?

My response, of course, was, 'Yeah.'

One of the men arguing against exclaimed: 'Have you seen the size of some of these women? If you put those women in shorts, it'll be unsightly.'

I answered, 'Have you seen the size of some of these men? Is the sight of them in shorts "unsightly"?'

It became a demonstration of a battle of the genders before finally, the case was resolved. There was no logical reason to prevent women from wearing shorts. From that point on, women tram conductors were permitted to wear shorts.

I loved my time as a tram conductor. I loved a good chitchat; it helped me improve my English. I had regular commuters who liked to tell me about their day, just passing time. Some were lonely, I imagine. I tried to make each journey conversational with topical subjects and current affairs. I did not have a boss. I thoroughly enjoyed this position and its freedoms, at times motioning to men in suits to stand for women with prams or shopping bags or assist them on and off the tram. I looked out for those most in need: pregnant women or women with children, the elderly, and people with disabilities. I engaged with all manner of everyday people: white collars, mothers, older women, homeless people, everyone. I would sometimes pull the cord to stop the tram between stops or hold back to let slower-moving people on.

Not long after the shorts incident, tram conductors went on strike over cost-cutting measures the Government sought to introduce. For weeks, trams were parked idle in the city centre. This meant we were not getting paid. While I respected and supported the cause, I also needed to earn a living. Being financially dependent on work, I had no choice but to find new means of providing for myself.

I searched again for employment, and several women's refuge adverts caught my eye. I applied.

❀   ❀   ❀

It was the late 1980s. I turned up to the job interview in my conductor's uniform—shorts, of course. The panel was curious as to why, and I explained the story. The interview proceeded with questions about my background and motivation, understanding of domestic violence and ways to intervene. I was offered employment as a support worker. To this day, I remember the joy and pride, the feeling of accomplishment I felt upon being validated as a worthy contributor to supporting women. To me, it meant all my life's traumas had not been in vain: these horrendous chapters would facilitate my support of others. I was also entering a space where women were in charge, making decisions, implementing them, all for the benefit of women. This was also a step away from my family's conventional employment.

After a few weeks of training, I took my first call from a woman in crisis. Talking to women leaving abusive homes came easy to me. They often had children and needed accommodation and support. I felt a rapport with them, and they were comforted by my reassuring voice. Essentially, our task was to get these women *out* of their (at times) dangerous living situations and *in* to some place safe. Of course, there was a deeply personal reason for why I gravitated to this kind of work, which gave my early days in the women's collective a deep sense of meaning and fulfilment. It seemed ideal—finding the solution not only to mine but to the world's problems.

I rapidly realised the flaws, limitations, and inadequacies of our service provision. Funding for women's services has never been a sustained priority, which limited our scope of intervention and support. Government support was always insufficient. It was part of an inadequate system responding to violence against women; set up to band-aid the problem, patch women up, and send them home.

One major issue that I quickly realised was the lack of insight about women's diversity, particularly in terms of ethnicity and culture. Our responses and support at times appeared as a blanket approach rather than a nuanced, tailored one. Although everyone working in the women's refuges was capable of providing support, we also came with different areas of expertise—as derived from our respective backgrounds. This resource, in my opinion, was not effectively utilised nor encouraged. For instance, surely my ability to speak Arabic put me in a more convenient position to support other Arabic-speaking women. Further, my perspective was shaped by lived experience, whereas some of my colleagues were tied to a more theoretical understanding of how best to support women in crisis.

Another limitation of our interventions was that our response to domestic violence remained largely—at the time—guided by concepts, rather than lived experience. I recall one training scenario where a hypothetical question was posed to me: 'A woman with two children calls you from a phone box. She has nowhere to go—all the refuges and accommodations are full. What do you tell her?'

The 'acceptable' answer would have been, 'There is nowhere for you to go.' Instead, I answered, 'There is always an option. I would go and pick her up and take her some place safe. We'd find another solution in the morning.'

For this response, I was told I had boundary issues that I needed to keep in check.

I understood the intention was to protect workers and our wellbeing, but I also knew the flip side of this reality. What might have happened if that woman spent a night on the street with her children? Perhaps from a non-lived experience, this was an acceptable reality—after all, the woman in this scenario had *left* the initial source of violence. But from a lived experience, this absence of support would force her back into the home. She would have to face either the violence she knows, or the unknown threat of being alone with her children in an unsafe environment. And she would have to make these difficult decisions while grappling with heightened levels of fear and anxiety.

These personal experiences could have enriched the organisation and our support. But the system was probably not ready nor was there political will to push the boundaries of our understanding for what support for the diversity of women escaping violence could look like.

It was in women's services that I first developed an understanding of the history and plight of First Nations peoples. I gravitated toward the staff of an Aboriginal women's refuge in Melbourne and the causes they championed, and learnt what it meant to be an ally to First Nations peoples.

My commitment to supporting First Nations women grew, not as a mere *ad hoc* endeavour, but rather, as a responsibility that accompanies me wherever I go. I found it confronting and disappointing to bear witness to the racism among women, and that they could not see the glaringly obvious injustice.

It was early in my time in the women's service sector that I first encountered inspirational women like Jackie Huggins and Lisa Thorpe. These women formed the early basis of my alliance with First Nations women.

During my time in women's services, I worked in various capacities; from direct service delivery, to providing support and counselling to women who had experienced the brutality of sexual assault and violence, to sitting on State and Federal committees and advisory groups. One of these group's focus was law reform around domestic abuse. At that time, men were able to use the judicial system to further their abuse. They had several legal avenues and defences in domestic violence cases, including the fact that women who sought to leave violence were mandated to undertake counselling; or that 'provocation' was an acceptable defence.

❋ ❋ ❋

I feel it is important I make a clear distinction between men who cause harm and those who stand as allies in our collective endeavour to the eradication of violence against women and children. I am not labelling men as inherently bad nor casting women solely as victims. Instead, I want to highlight that men often benefit from privileges embedded in social systems, and with those privileges arises their responsibility. Societies also reinforce and uphold attitudes that grant men permission and entitlement over the lives of women and girls. We all need to work towards shifting attitudes to eradicate violence against women and children.

Crucially, it is also important not to reinforce cultural stereotypes. Violence toward women is a pervasive epidemic, not confined by geographic or cultural boundaries. Its eradication requires a collective commitment on a global scale.

❈ ❈ ❈

I was still only twenty-five and I needed to have greater legal knowledge for my evolving roles. I enrolled at university in a combined arts and law degree. My elective subjects centred around law, feminism, sociology and criminology. My motivation was to gain understanding of the laws which govern the responses to violence against women.

My studies drew me closer to the voices which had been muted: First Nations peoples'. I sought to centre their experiences and understand their relationship to the law. I drew on what I had learnt from Lowitja O'Donoghue, Shirley Coleen Smith, Essie Coffey, and Gladys Elphik, all of whom tirelessly contributed to the advancement of First Nations peoples' rights. These remarkable women were united in a common cause—empowering Indigenous women through education as an investment in the strength and resilience of their communities. Their work and advocacy is key to creating a future where equity and justice prevail.

These women have been instrumental in laying the foundations for change. They should be better known— should be celebrated for their work in improving the health and welfare of First Nations peoples and for the part they played in setting up legal services, community outreach, and drafting of the *Native Title Act*.

I spent fifteen years in women's services. I developed

knowledge and understanding of the system and sector responsible for supporting women. During this time, I also identified its deficits and limitations in responding to some of the most marginalised women's needs.

Working in these spaces also became a way for me to work through some of my own issues and trauma and helped me address some of the residual impacts of those years of being married. I felt I had found my calling in life—supporting others, especially those most vulnerable, and affecting change in their lives. A motto I worked and lived by: 'When you support and lift up women, you progress the entire society.' It was an incredibly healing place for everyone who participated; from the management to the staff, and to the women seeking our support.

The staff of the women's crisis services should be thanked for all their work and unwavering commitment to ensuring the safety of women and children. I feel a strong sense of duty to complement this work, providing support where such organisations cannot.

❈ ❈ ❈

Outside of work, I learnt to live on very little—after all, I had some training in poverty's ways. I bought a house on a whim with no money and no planning.

One very hot summer day, the sky was particularly bright, and I had forgotten my sunglasses at home. On my way to meet a friend for coffee, the sun's bright reflection bounced off a sign that read 'OPEN FOR INSPECTION' displayed on the footpath outside a leaning Edwardian bungalow (it was evident the house was tilted to the left).

Curiously, I approached the front door. The agent did not think much about my presence. In fact, as I asked a few questions, he exclaimed, 'You are not a serious buyer.'

I replied, 'Don't make assumptions.'

I'm not sure why I needed to walk through this house. He followed me in and insisted that if I was serious, I'd place a written offer. Which, to my surprise, I did.

I borrowed the deposit of five per cent from a friend and obtained mortgage insurance for the remainder, as I had no credit history to my name and being a woman made it difficult to get a loan without this extra expense.

I was beginning to build my new life for myself, on my own terms. My days, notwithstanding the grief and loss of my boys, became a joy, save for the legal battle surrounding custody of my children. Even on the toughest of days I knew that I was happier in my freedom than I had ever been within the confines of my married life.

REUNION

Mid-1990s. A knock on the door. Here they were, my sons, as though by magic, standing before me after what felt like an eternity of separation. Their innocent eyes, tender and confused, seeking a mother's comfort, were searching for answers which even I could not provide. The injustice of being stripped away from them, the pain of that moment, still resides deep within my soul, a reminder of the yearning that permeated my existence for so long. They were now two teenagers. Their faces were immediately recognisable, even after years apart. Their essence had remained etched in my heart all this time. The tears flowed uncontrollably.

I pulled them into a warm embrace. The weight of their absence dissolved. They walked into my heart—a place that had always remained theirs. I provided a safe home where they could find their mother's love, acceptance, and safety. We fumbled our way through this surreal, long-awaited reunion. Our lives were now intertwined again; defined by our lengthy separation, love, compassion, and yearning. From now on, we would be determined to make the most of every precious moment we had together.

They were young strangers, transformed by life with their father and my absence. I was equally a stranger to them. Yet they knew to come home to me once they could. The journey was not easy—transitioning to becoming a family once more required us to learn to know each other, to learn to trust each other, and to learn to communicate in relatable ways.

I organised house meetings to introduce them to the idea that they could raise any concerns and issues they had, and they would always be heard. With that arrangement, the responsibility and therefore the decision-making stopped with me.

I also re-experienced the simple pleasures of their company. We existed in the unspoken understanding of our once-estranged family. In their return, I understood the fleeting nature of time and the enduring nature of a mother's love—a reminder that even in the midst of life's greatest uncertainties, there is *always* hope, always possibility. Love, respect, and open communication guided us through the trials yet to come, knowing that together we could overcome anything, just as we had resolved the impact and anguish of separation.

Amidst the profound joy that accompanied their return, I also recognise the utmost significance of safeguarding their privacy. One thing is clear: their stories are theirs alone to tell, not to be included as part of mine. Each of us possesses a unique set of experiences, emotions, and reflections which shape our identities and define our lives. Just as my own story is sacred to me, I understand that both my boys, now fully grown men, deserve the same reverence and protection for their personal lives. In a world often enamoured with exposure, I appreciate the importance of allowing my sons to set the boundaries of their own privacy. The decision to share their personal journeys should never be forced nor compromised.

MOROCCAN
SOUP BAR

BIRTH OF THE MOROCCAN SOUP BAR

One late Thursday afternoon in 1998, I found myself in a state of complete exasperation and frustration after a difficult day at work—we had failed to provide support to a woman escaping violence because she did not meet the criteria for crisis accommodation. I had exhausted every avenue to no avail. To me, this was deeply personal, as I had a lived experience of domestic violence: it strips victims of their dignity and confidence and undermines their very sense of self.

Stuck in traffic on my way home, I looked across the road, my eyes fixed on a shop front displaying a 'FOR LEASE' sign. I felt a tug in my heart, calling me to stop and check this place out.

Without a second thought, I pulled over, jumped out, and dialled the real estate agent's number. The agent, as luck would have it, was just around the corner and was happy to meet. While I waited, my mind wandered, taking me into another realm of dreams and possibilities. I began picturing a space for women, a haven, where women could be themselves. An environment where they could not only escape the clutches of crisis and disadvantage, but also *thrive*. It would be a place of women, for women, by women.

I wanted a space that would sustainably complement some of the limitations of women's services, accessible to victims of domestic violence—a circuit-breaker to the cycle of crisis for women, and in particular, for women on the margins. I imagined the walls of this vacant space coming alive with storytelling, cooking, pickling—I wasn't yet sure.

As my imagination took hold of me, the real estate agent arrived. To my surprise, I found myself negotiating the terms of a lease. Rent free for three months, plus a twenty per cent discount for the first year—I do love a good haggle. I danced my way through the shop front.

And just like that, 183 St Georges Road, Fitzroy North became the birth of the Moroccan Soup Bar. A blank canvas of hope and possibility.

Little did I know that this serendipitous encounter with a 'FOR LEASE' sign would change my life.

From that moment on, a new journey began. I did not know yet what we would become, how it would work, or what would we do. Would I bring women in? To do what? Armed only with my convictions and dreams for a better tomorrow, perhaps I could bring a taste of Moroccan hospitality to Fitzroy North.

My thoughts ran rampant. I needed to focus, so I asked myself a few questions centred around women and their needs: What are women great at? How do we reach women at great social disadvantage? How do we support them to overcome a life of violence? How do we best advocate for them and for their needs?

No matter the cultural group, women have been socially conditioned to occupy kitchens, a trait too often used as a tool for control. Rarely has this conditioning been accessed as a source of support. Yet, I wondered what would happen if we subverted this and turned subjugation on its head: Let's use the kitchen as the means to walk alongside women on their journey of transformation. It should be that simple.

I wondered what the outcome for women in need of a better life would be. That they were recognised and paid for their contributions as cooks, cleaners, hospitality providers? In fact, often these everyday home duties come at the cost of their own desires, needs, hopes, and dreams. Validating women via employment became the foundational pillar of the Moroccan Soup Bar.

The first major problem we tackled was domestic violence.

To enter a refuge, women were required to forgo any support they may have had: they could not have any contact with siblings, friends, or extended family. These conditions created further isolation to already marginalised women, who did not necessarily speak the dominant language nor fit into the dominant culture. And once these women *leave* refuge, their support needs are complex and numerous, from immigration to income to housing issues (to name a few).

Women needed the resources to rebuild independent lives. The smallest amount of financial support provided was never enough to sustain a family. Crucially, at the Moroccan Soup Bar, we responded to the immediate need for employment without invalidating women's experiences. We spoke to the practical and psychological impact of leaving violence and offered education and staff development in a way that did not compete with women being able to put food on the table. This was doubly important for single-income households. Our working model has developed organically with each woman's needs informing our response.

Today, domestic violence statistics are, if not the same, worse than when I left the women's sector. All the social issues are still present. One or more women every week are being killed at the hands of a partner she knows, and yet our rhetoric is filled with claims of gender safety, equality, and respect. I have come to confront the notion that women need to leave their abuser several times before they are finally 'ready' to leave. In the twenty-five years since establishing the Moroccan Soup Bar, no woman has returned to an abusive home. This reality challenges the notion of a revolving-door scenario. Women only leave numerous times because the alternatives on offer are largely inadequate to their needs, and to a life of safety and independence. Women leave to circuit-break the crisis, but they go back because there is no continuity of care that is meaningful and relevant to them.

Over the years, themes emerged in the women seeking employment and support. Different groups of women needed tailored responses from their employment, and different groups accessed employment for different reasons. Initially, our focus was on women escaping violence. Post September 11, a different cohort of women sought out support: Muslim women who found themselves on the receiving end of Islamophobia, which transpired in numerous ways, including barriers to employment and heightened fear of public violence against them.

They recognised themselves in the Moroccan Soup Bar's environment and our underpinning foundations. They felt safe and validated in our spaces. The focus was on their personal safety in public, acknowledging the sustained discrimination and abuse they endured in the public realm. Islamophobia was being acutely felt by women and at times put women in harm's way, particularly those with obvious Muslim dress codes. They were the easiest, softest targets of cowardly acts of violence that occurred daily.

The women's experiences enabled us to develop ways to remove the barriers that hindered their paths to safety and autonomy. This included daily conversations around safety measures, sending two staff members together to go shopping, setting up a phone tree to contact one another, checking in at the end of each day, setting up dialogue with the local police station, and, very importantly, sharing this reality with our customers.

❀   ❀   ❀

When I established the Moroccan Soup Bar, I was not known in the hospitality scene. While there are still many systemic inequalities today, twenty-five years ago, the hospitality industry was just not made for women nor supportive of our initiative. Business was dominated by men who enjoyed status and were afforded celebrity. As a woman entering this domain, I had to learn about operating a business with no guidance, no mentors, and little support networks.

Navigating this complex and often inaccessible new environment was daunting. Yet, it was exhilarating, as I could defy expectations and create my very own version of hospitality. No bank would fund me on the basis that, 'I know in my very being that this will work'. No produce suppliers would set up an account for me on trust alone, which meant the Moroccan Soup Bar could not live on borrowed money. I needed to show credit history, a business plan, industry references, of which I had none. The fact that I had 'a woman's hunch' was not enough.

I decided to open as soon as I had collected enough furniture to fill the space. After being rejected for a bank loan, I went to thrift shops and bought the tables and chairs—some rickety and barely standing. I bought things second-hand, and arranged them with a sense of pride. Having done a lot of physical work throughout my life, I found myself quite capable.

Despite their scepticism at the time, family and friends were also put to work. My father helped me make the paint in the same way it was done in Morocco, creating vibrant colours to cover our walls and furniture. The front counter was donated to me by a friend's mother who worked in a lingerie shop. I constructed a timber top, polished, and painted in a deep teal. It was made with love and added so much warmth to our new space.

I was, at times, apprehensive. I worried about customers not turning up, or, worse, rejecting our vision. Yet I had the inner drive and determination to continue, as the stakes were too high—I wanted to change the world!

All in all, armed with an accidental lease on a property in Fitzroy North, I stuck with my conviction and took down the paper covering the front window to reveal the words 'Moroccan Soup Bar'. As a child, I did not belong to Lebanon or Australia, but through my heritage, I had developed an internal identity as a Moroccan, where I anchored my hope of freedom.

I opened the front door and waited, standing in the middle of this new restaurant with vibrant colours, rickety chairs, and eclectic furniture, all bathed in the aromas of my childhood kitchen. Here I was, looking cool and calm on the outside, but inside I was dizzy with stage fright.

I kept asking myself if someone was going to come in. The cook and the waitress stood behind the counter, similarly nervous in anticipation. Suddenly, distracted thoughts emerged: *How will we figure out our opening hours? What will people think of our spoken menu?*

Our first two customers walked in. I guided them to a table. They asked about our menu and prices. I answered, 'Now let's see … we have soups! Dips, and soups, dips, soups, and soups and dips. The soup is $4.50, and soup and dips are $5.50.'

It *was* just soups and dips, initially: harira soup, spinach and lentil, yellow lentil, and mint noodle. Four soups, a range of mezze, and some dips. We only had a small domestic stove in the kitchen, which limited our offerings.

The customers trickled in—a couple, one person on their own, then two, then one … 'We're getting busy!' I exclaimed.

With a few people seated, we realised we had not anticipated how the orders would be plated. Our first order of the day—harira soup and dips—was served on chunky ceramic crockery replicating Moroccan aesthetics. It certainly looked and *smelled* appetising. We placed a bowl of soup atop a plate with some mezze dips—roasted capsicum, hummus—and garnished it with sweet paprika and parsley, served with a chunky piece of sourdough bread. This became the way we presented our soup dishes: telling the story of warmth and hospitality that we wanted to convey through hearty and delectable food.

On this special first day, an older man—I never learnt his name—asked a lot of questions. He wanted to know about me, my motivation, my vision. I sensed his curiosity was different from other customers'. He was a true gentleman, softly spoken. He ordered a selection of our sweets and a mint tea. He devoured the meal, motioned me back to him, and took out a $100 note from his wallet. He said, 'Good luck to you.'

Overwhelmed, I tried to refuse—for me, $100 would feed a family of four for a week! But he insisted, 'I like your vibe. I want to support you and your business.'

I still have the $100 note, as I cherished the sentiment and symbol of his support. It was a testament to the people who believed in the Moroccan Soup Bar's unconventional vibes and our story and community. This random act of generosity reinforced to me the notion that as long as our idea resonates even with one person, we can be satisfied.

The first day of service went smoothly. Customers left happy and well fed. We closed the door, feeling content, exhausted, and reassured. Some people came and enjoyed our proposition. I called my mother, ecstatically, to tell her, 'We made $180!'

Over the following week, more people came, and then more the week after that. Soon we were full every day. The level of curiosity for the Moroccan Soup Bar was almost instantaneous.

Our spoken menu, while it *was* meant to replicate the experience of being at a café in Morocco, it was also that, at the time of opening, we simply did not have the money to print menus.

'Is there a menu?'

'Yes, it's spoken!'

This became a defining feature of the Moroccan Soup Bar, so popular that even when we could afford to print, I insisted on keeping the menu spoken.

As we grew in popularity, it was impractical to have to repeat the menu a hundred times each night—as much as I love to talk, that was too many spoken words, even for me. Instead, and in an effort to break down barriers, I encouraged people to sit together, share tables, meet and greet, which would allow me to explain the menu fewer times. And thus, communal dining was born out of a spoken menu.

Good evening, and welcome to the Moroccan Soup Bar.

How many of you have dined with us before? Show of hands. The Moroccan Soup Bar is founded on the values of what we call open hospitality, mindful of the land and the place upon which we stand, and our impact on the environment in which we live. Our aim is to break the cycle of disadvantage for women through employment as well as to provide safe spaces for those who find themselves recipients of prejudice and hostility.

> *It is she who changes attitudes,*
> *It is she who progresses society,*
> *It is she who will change the world.*
> *In our spaces, women flourish.*

The girls will be with you shortly to speak the menu. Enjoy your evening.

THE WOMEN

Within the confines of the vibrant yellow, tangerine and teal-painted walls of our restaurant, something *new* was taking shape. An environment that centred and celebrated the hospitality, generosity, community, talent, and resilience of women on the margins of society. The Moroccan Soup Bar has evolved into a place where women are empowered and not judged; where they can pray if they want (even in the middle of a busy shift) and wear what they choose. The Moroccan Soup Bar is an unofficial place for women to transition to independence.

Every woman who works at the Moroccan Soup Bar is woven into the very fabric of its community. While their stories are unique, there exists a thread of shared experiences that often unites women on the margins of society. Whether they are facing personal crises or navigating societal disadvantage, these remarkable women often found solace and support within the safe walls of the Moroccan Soup Bar, their contributions enriching our communities.

When I think about this, one such remarkable woman comes to mind. Her story resonates deeply, serving as a symbol of inspiration to me and the many lives she touched at the Moroccan Soup Bar.

One early evening, as we prepared for the dinner service—responding to messages left on the answering machine, trying to beat the six o'clock opening deadline, the queue growing outside our door—a woman made her way to the front of the queue and knocked on the door.

With remarkable courage and purposeful intent, she made her way in, her tall, elegant frame filling the doorway. No room for small talk or niceties—she, armed with little English—slapped me on the back, squeezed my shoulder, and demanded, 'I want a job.' Her two very young children were in tow.

I asked her if she was okay, and if she could come back to see me the following day, outside of service hours.

She replied, 'I want a job now! My children want food. I want a job to get a house.'

My Somali was bad, and she spoke little English. At that time, we had another Somalian-speaking worker who intervened and translated.

This woman had nowhere to stay, she had just left a violent marriage, and had been sleeping in her car with her two children. We ensured she was safe, organised accommodation for a few nights, provided food, and asked her to come in the next day to start work. This typified the extent of our interview process; a woman just came in and asked!

I knew too well the circumstances which drive women to this level of despair. The emotional language of desperate turmoil crosses cultural and linguistic boundaries. While the specific circumstances may differ, it feels the same, no matter where you come from.

Having fled from violence with her two children, this woman was left with absolutely no belongings other than the clothes on their backs. She was a fiercely protective mother, searching for ways to keep her children safe, fed, and with somewhere safe and warm to sleep.

The days turned into weeks, then months, then years. She moved into long-term housing and worked with us for many years, becoming a member of our extended family. She now works as an unapologetic advocate for women and girls in her community. When she comes across a woman in need, she calls me. I am always happy to hear from her and provide practical support for the women she sends my way. She was not a victim, but a capable woman who could contribute—not just to her own survival but also to the community that would embrace her.

Her story is one of many examples of the women who became catalysts for change. Encouraged by her example, others sought out support and changed their lives. And thus, the impact of her courage rippled outward, transforming the lives of all of us who found ourselves lucky enough to be in her orbit.

This is not unusual. While cultures are diverse, a common factor remains: the control of women through social norms and laws. The Moroccan Soup Bar is a space where women's experiences are validated, their voices are heard, and their potential is nurtured.

Another employee found herself entangled in a situation she could not resolve alone. She had recently joined the Moroccan Soup Bar as one of our cooks. She had a keen interest in cooking and hospitality and was eager to learn the ropes so that she might make a successful career in this industry someday.

However, her aspirations were overshadowed by a 'cultural' tradition deeply ingrained in her family: her aunt, who she respected and loved, had arranged for her to marry a man from overseas who she neither knew nor wanted to marry. This was justified under the guise of 'tradition'; insisting that it was in her best interest to be married. She was overcome by guilt, especially as she had deep respect for her aunt who had taken her into her home when she migrated to Australia and provided her with shelter and safety in a foreign country. She was torn between the need to please and be grateful and the need to survive and be free. To me, she expressed her reluctance to marry this man, and her ambivalence around familial and cultural expectations.

I knew firsthand the harm that a forced arranged marriage could inflict upon her. Determined to find a solution, we contacted our connections in the Immigration Department, as we were, at times, in touch about the circumstances of some of our employees. I explained this woman's current predicament, including the lack of consent to her marriage, and the situation was subsequently investigated. This put a resounding end to her ordeal.

She continued her work at the Moroccan Soup Bar, where she received professional development and personal support, as she worked towards her independence.

Her story, too, had a ripple effect and inspired other women. They were encouraged to question long-held beliefs, customs, and traditions that perpetuate control and condone violence, and to reject traditions founded on deep-seated inequality that denied women personal agency. However small the outward effect of her story, it led to a shift in attitudes within some of our staff, creating new traditions and greater recognition for women's autonomy. In particular, the power for women to make choices about their own lives.

❋ ❋ ❋

On a cool Melbourne day, one of our staff arrived at work wearing a high-necked top—a departure from her usual attire. Curious, the others greeted her, questioning her choice to cover up. She explained that the chill in the air prompted her to stay warm.

Amidst the laughter and banter, one of our staff exclaimed, 'Looks like it's time we got some heating in here.'

We all chuckled at the irony.

This story is about more than just a change in wardrobe. It is about a woman who walked into our restaurant and into our lives and immediately charmed us with her infectious laughter and joyful personality. She was someone truly special. The staff took an immediate liking to her, insisting that she be hired on the spot. And she was.

As the days passed, it became evident that she had left her previous job because she couldn't conform to their expectations. Apparently, her choice of clothing, which occasionally revealed a hint of cleavage, was deemed inappropriate by her employer.

But here, we saw things differently. We understood that her cleavage was not a liability. To her, dressing in this way was a natural part of her femininity. To the women of the Soup Bar, this was seen as a gift from God. They agreed that her breasts should be blessed and appreciated, even celebrated.

She filled our workplace with a sense of light-heartedness and joy. Everyone looked forward to coming to work when she was around. She fitted in perfectly and we learnt a lot from each other.

These women's experiences serve as a reminder that they are not alone in their struggles and that together, they can find the resources, support, and resilience to start anew.

Accepting and celebrating women for who they are, creating the conditions where they can thrive and where their best expressions can be realised, are measures of our success. While these and other stories indicate a harmonious workplace, there were also testing and challenging times. One particular incident springs to mind.

In 2005, Australia introduced a set of sedition laws. One of the first direct consequences of these laws was even greater suspicion and surveillance of Muslim women.

Some of our staff were uncomfortable with the added attention this drew to our workplace, as one of our staff—a devout Muslim—wore a niqab. So tense was this atmosphere and anxiety that, ultimately, they could not bear the added scrutiny they felt was brought onto their lives.

Some of the women approached me to voice their concerns, as they could not continue to endure the stress and worry and asked for relief. Perhaps she could take some time off, or maybe remove her niqab?

This situation presented a dilemma. Would we cower to the fear of public hostility? Would we sacrifice some of the most vulnerable among us? Although this angst was very real for our staff—they were justified in not wanting added attention on their lives—wearing a niqab was also this woman's right and entitlement.

After much discussion, individually and collectively and with an emphasis on education and support without judgment, the situation was resolved and the staff stood by her.

It is in these moments that our convictions, our values, our integrity, and the very foundation of the Moroccan Soup Bar are tested. We have a responsibility to care for those who are vulnerable and not to punish them further.

❁ ❁ ❁

Another moment feels important to mention—one that demonstrates the importance of providing access to information and support.

The public discourse on female genital mutilation (FGM) intensified in the community when the Government mandated reporting any such practice and or intent to practice.

At the time, we had staff from the Horn of Africa where FGM is commonly performed. I asked a Somalian colleague from the women's sector to provide education and training to our staff, using various hypothetical scenarios. In one of those scenarios, a woman was convinced that FGM would benefit her daughter, render her marriageable, and help her transcend her place in society. This scenario was discussed by the group, contested, challenged, and importantly, placed back in context of history and traditions.

When asked *why* some women might want their daughters to undergo this procedure, someone explained, 'Because it is a requirement of their religion.'

'Their religion is *my* religion,' I answered. 'I have read

the Quran, and nothing in the Quran requires women to undertake such brutal practices. Female genital mutilation is not an Islamic tradition but is a method whereby men exert control over women and their bodies.'

These events gave the women permission to question, understand, and explore the origin and impact of such practices in a safe environment. We debunked some of the myths, and rediscovered women's rights within a faith-based context. The women gained insight and knowledge, which only strengthened their rejection of any such practices that brutalise and violate women.

These conversations spilled over from the workplace, into homes, and into the greater community. We've heard on the grapevine that some of these women have continued to advocate for women's rights in this way, encouraging others in their footsteps.

❀   ❀   ❀

Once a woman leaves refuge, one of the main difficulties she faces is trying to find a house. Public housing often requires being placed on a waiting list for several years, forcing women into the private rental market. Both the costs and requirements for private rental properties are often insurmountable, especially without a reference or an existing lease in your name (something that is often withheld by abusive partners as a method of exerting control). Over time, we have come to develop personal relationships with some of our patrons, including people who work in real estate. When the need arose, I would reach out to them and offer up the Moroccan Soup Bar as guarantor or referee on their behalf. This at least provided them with equal opportunity to enter the private rental market.

❀   ❀   ❀

Women are creative, flexible, and innovative. At times, they would make their own arrangements and organise to live together to combine the families' costs, including prohibitive childcare costs. Some women exchanged the child-minding role—genius!—and organised their work schedules around shared child-minding responsibilities.

'I'll look after your kids when you're at work, and then you can look after mine?'

They took advantage of the opportunity to create their own sense of family. They validated one another and replaced a would-be sense of isolation with connection and strong bonds.

I would often hear them say to one another:

'You're like me, we have a similar background.'

'We're not going back—let's kick him out for good!'

These are practical examples of what can be achieved in a trusted ecosystem.

That said, if *abusers* were held truly accountable for their coercion, control and violence against women, perhaps things would be different. As it currently stands, the trauma falls on women and their dependents to upend their lives following domestic violence. Why couldn't it be the other way around, whereby they get to stay in the home, provided protection to ensure their safety? Shouldn't *women* be given the opportunity to thrive again?

Perhaps the removal of abusers, shifting the onus of starting anew onto *them*, should be actively considered.

❈ ❈ ❈

Over the years, the Moroccan Soup Bar has become a community hub, interwoven with stories of celebration, resilience, hope and social engagement. We have transcended the boundaries of culture and religion, symbolising hope and unity for our community. We not only defy societal conventions but also provided a space for women to reclaim their lives, their autonomy, and their authentic expression. Our measures of success extend beyond conventional notions of profit and fame. For us, success means creating meaningful impact in the lives of the women we employ.

Good evening, and welcome to the Moroccan Soup Bar.

Take a moment, look around, say hi to a stranger (at least for tonight).

I've been thinking about the importance of nurturing communities. Every night at the Moroccan Soup bar, we come together not only to share a meal but also a sense of belonging. Our diversity is a cause for celebration, and everyone plays a role in creating a supportive environment. Together, by ensuring everyone is treated with dignity and respect, we form a stronger, kinder, and more compassionate community.

Tonight, we are showcasing our new tapas shared banquet.

THE CUSTOMERS

I have been vegetarian for most of my life. As the main cook, I curated a vegetarian menu that merged traditional flavours and vegetarian cuisine with a contemporary twist. I adapted the chickpea bake (fatteh) which was one of our eight main meals, and this became the centrepiece of our menu. It is a dish enjoyed across the Middle East and North Africa, originating in humble homes, where old stale bread found new life. Some variations incorporated meats, while ours catered to vegetarians by transforming chickpeas into a satisfying meal.

The chickpea bake has a tale of its own to tell. With a cult-like following, its devotees craved its intricate flavours and textures. The burnt butter turned the baked bread into a nutty taste sensation, elevating it to legendary status on our menu. Some likened it to an orchestra in the mouth, some described as a dance on the palate, and others named it the 'velvety smooth crispy crunch'.

But perhaps the true magic of the chickpea bake lies in its ability to bring people together—united by their love of food and the joy of sharing a meal, longing for just one more bite.

I have told stories many times from the life of the Moroccan Soup Bar. Here I will tell some of them again.

❊ ❊ ❊

Ramadan is a holy month in which Muslims observe introspection and transcend the need for immediate gratification. One of its expressions is fasting from dusk to dawn, and breaking the daily fasting—Iftar—with family and in community.

On one of these evenings, a transgender woman entered the dining room. The way she carried herself made the customers stop and stare. She strode into the restaurant alone, with elegance and poise. She was the embodiment of confidence and self-assuredness. I directed her to a table.

Two other women came in, also wanting a table. One of them wore a niqab. As I glanced across the dining room for seating that would be appropriate to them, the woman wearing the niqab made her way to where the transgender woman was and asked if they could join her.

It was at this table that she felt able to remove her face covering. This situation was a striking juxtaposition, yet there was an undeniable sense of comfort and empathy between them. Both women felt a sense of ease in the other's company—a display of the unspoken acknowledgment of each other's struggles. They shared stories over a meal.

Before parting ways, they exchanged phone numbers; a tangible sign of their newfound friendship. I couldn't help but be curious and moved by their bond. In their unlikely encounter, I found affirmation of the power of human interaction, a symbol of hope.

❈ ❈ ❈

The Moroccan Soup Bar has a recognisable buzz, reminiscent of the bustling atmosphere of a souk. It is vibrant, lively, and loud. With the proximity of each table and communal dining, people from all walks of life engage in conversation. They often leave with the feeling of being nourished and enriched by the human connections formed. At times, they might also leave feeling challenged.

Around 7.30pm, the Moroccan Soup Bar was full. At one of the tables, a man had opened a can of beer. I immediately attended the table and explained that alcohol consumption was not permitted, as we did not hold a liquor licence.

In response, the man shouted, 'You want to turn this country into a fucking Islamic state?'

His outburst brought the room to an abrupt silence. I felt mortified. I gathered my composure and responded, 'I'm not sure I possess that level of power, mate. You think I can dictate an entire country's belief system?'

I then attended to another table, checked their allergies, and their hunger level (we used a hunger scale to determine how much food to bring out). I explained the menu, all the while being aware of the man's table.

I noticed he appeared to be calmer and did not open another drink. He and his friends ate all their food.

When the time came to settle the bill for the group, the man walked up to the register alone. His demeanour had changed, he was more tempered. When he requested the bill, I told him his meal was for free. I wanted to show him who we were, and how wrong his assumptions were. Fighting bigotry with generosity.

He protested, and I insisted, urging him to embrace this expression of our hospitality. He eventually agreed, extended his hand to shake mine, and told me his name was Dave.

Dave came back to the restaurant a few weeks later with his friends.

He wanted to talk with me before being seated, perhaps to check he was welcomed back. After they sat down, he said to his friends, 'You can't drink here, but the tucker is good.' I joined them for a chat during their dinner.

Oftentimes, there is a pathway to resolution, by finding commonalities. This was an important lesson for me and my staff, and no doubt for him.

❋ ❋ ❋

The walls of the Moroccan Soup Bar were gradually filled over the years as customers donated artworks. A mysterious artist painted unique caricatures of me—his expression spoke to our changing times. Each piece held a cherished place on the walls. I would have them laminated and proudly displayed for all to see. I eagerly anticipated meeting this anonymous stranger, the annual ritual, and their insights. They remained a mystery until one day, Mikko—the artist—stood at the counter. Softly spoken, bothered by the troubles of the world, he was as I had imagined him: a medieval treasure.

He continues to paint, and I eagerly anticipate his next surprise. I feel a profound sense of appreciation and gratitude to Mikko. Thank you for the two decades of inspiration. Through your art, you have become an integral part of our history and community.

❋ ❋ ❋

Every evening, a few customers would receive a meal on

the house as a gesture of our hospitality. It could have been for students who were less able to afford a healthy meal than others, for someone's birthday, for a discussion we shared, and sometimes it was just a matter of 'why not?' Every time, people protested, as if this act of generosity could not be accepted. And in our banter, I would ask them to extend this kindness and give the money to someone in need on their travels.

One night, a young man came in and asked for me by name, wanting to thank me. I found this curious, as I did not recognise him. He went on to explain: For a time, he had found himself in difficult situations, and homeless. A passer-by approached him with a bank note and said, 'This is from the women at the Moroccan Soup Bar.' He was puzzled. Although a small amount of money for many, this, to him, was both practically necessary and a symbol of care. With it, he could afford accommodation for the night.

When his circumstances changed for the better, he decided to come in, wanting to understand and thank us for passing on this warm gesture. In his words, the kindness of strangers made him feel less alone and a little more hopeful.

We never know the rippling effects of acts of generosity.

Good evening, and welcome to the Moroccan Soup Bar.

Dining at the Moroccan Soup Bar is a conduit for meaningful conversations. We hold dear the principles of justice and fairness, and we recognise the importance of addressing social inequalities. We want to ensure that our spaces are respectful, equitable, and just for all. By providing support to the most marginalised among us, we create a more inclusive society. Speak to strangers, engage in conversations that celebrate and embrace our diversity, let us together reimagine what a society that values humanity can look like.

The girls will bring out the main courses soon.
We hope you enjoy your meal.

DINING

Each evening the Moroccan Soup Bar transforms into more than just a place to eat; it becomes a sanctuary, a haven where everyone feels accepted and valued. The Soup Bar stands as a testament to the power of a shared meal, where the flavours of social justice and compassion are just as important as the delectable dishes served.

Inside our humble eatery, the quest for a fulfilling dinner goes far beyond simply satisfying hunger. It is a feast for our community's soul.

My passion for social justice has intensified over the course of my life. The more our society becomes divisive and hostile to the vulnerable among us, the louder my voice is: inviting us to be better, to find strength in our differences rather than fear them. At the Moroccan Soup Bar, we have created new platforms of engagement around food and where people congregate, as well as establishing a business designed to circuit-break the cycle of disadvantage for women, providing avenues of empowerment and independence through employment. In doing so, we have also created a dining space that is respectful, welcoming, and safe to all.

Our aim is to nourish not only the bodies but also the souls of our patrons and communities. An important part of our service is an acknowledgement of our responsibility as benefactors working on unceded lands. We cannot advocate for a *little* bit of justice for *some* causes. Australia has never resolved its history with the original custodians; consequently, we all have a responsibility towards First Nations communities. We acknowledge the necessity of actively supporting First Nations peoples, both within our establishment and in the broader society.

True alliance demands more than ceremonial words of acknowledgment; it requires behavioural change, tangible outcomes, and responsible collaboration with First Nations peoples in all our endeavours. We invite our community to join in and advance these causes, thereby contributing to the ongoing process of genuine reconciliation. We actively engage with First Nations women's initiatives and work to foster spaces that respect and uplift Indigenous knowledge, culture, and sovereignty.

❀ ❀ ❀

In 2019, we opened a venue around the corner to ease the demand on our dining and take away. Located 500 meters up the road, the Moroccan Soup Bar Two-Go moved into an old building. The two-storey house was converted into separate dining spaces. The rooms were designed to engage with the contemporary tensions facing our society. Conversation starters tailored to the name and the themes of the room were delivered alongside meals, written on little cards left on the tables, each inviting our patrons to question assumptions and learn. Our customers embraced this concept—the rooms were often booked out in advance. People were clearly hungry for engagement.

The Kitchen and the Salon

These were two separate rooms for customers to dine, both of which have always been close to my heart. What happens in the kitchen transpires in the salon. Interweaving culinary and social aspects, this connection between the kitchen and salon has become a link across generations.

The kitchen, once private, has become a bridge rewriting the past and offering new customs to the present. Beyond recipes, the ingredients combine with tales of life, love, resilience, and celebration. The aroma leads from the kitchen's raw honesty to the formality of the salon, where traditions are dressed in etiquettes. In the salon, rituals with carefully chosen words and deliberate utterances create rules and traditions.

I would often suggest having a first dinner in the Kitchen and coming back for a second visit in the Salon. In both spaces, I was the storyteller, guiding diners from the home's core, the kitchen, to the salon's ambiance. Each night, hypotheticals were presented, and thought-provoking questions were posed. In the Kitchen, diners could discuss the origins of food and its sourcing, our relationship to ingredients, and the impact of food on our health and wellbeing. They would be empowered in the realisation that anyone can cook healthy, nutritious meals in a sustainable manner.

In the Salon, diners were invited to challenge formal societal etiquette, much of which reinforces and perpetuates social inequality.

The Women's Room

It will not come as a surprise to the reader that anyone can reel off a list of names of men who have contributed to the progressing of our societies. It is a much more difficult task to name significant women. Naturally, the Women's Room was dedicated to women's writings and their contributions to the betterment of our societies. We put out a call for donations of books written by women and they came flooding in. We built shelves to house hundreds of books by women authors. The walls were lined with writings across time and genre. The entire collection offered words and wisdoms, enveloping diners in the amazing legacies of women. Septima Clark, Angela Davis, Malala Yousafzai, Anita Heiss, amina wadud, Hannah Arendt, Fatma Mernissi, Arundhati Roy, Shirin Ebadi, Trin Minh Ha, Simone Weil, Virginie Despentes, Samah Sabawi, Randa Abdel Fattah, Sara Saleh, Helen Keller, Toni Morrisson, Claire Colman, Sally Morgan, Jane Harrrison, and Clementine Ford, to name a few. *A room of her own* came to life.

This small dining room invited patrons to acknowledge and celebrate the role of women in shaping and progressing our societies. It was open to everyone—an invitation to learn and engage with women's writings and stories.

The Boudoir

Dinning in the Boudoir invited the patrons to examine our understanding of intimacy and think about notions of consent. It provided an opportunity to delve into women's conditioning, and challenge men's sense of entitlement over women's minds and bodies. The boudoir was a room where strategically placed images prompted conversations and exploration.

'I am my own guardian'; a poster exploring the true meaning of guardianship and consent. This prop was initially designed as part of the Saudi Arabian women's liberation movement against guardianship laws, but its relevance is not lost in the boudoir space.

I also placed an old North African consent and fertility board. In old times, this board hung outside women's bedroom doors to signal their readiness for sexual intimacy. The notion of consent is not new. Women have been tussling with these issues for centuries. I often question why these rituals and practices did not endure.

With the pressure of social media in defining gender roles, we are witnessing a worrying trend, where we are reinforcing the subjugation of women. Instead of women's autonomy being secured, it seems women's agency is slowly being erased. Like many of the issues currently facing our societies, intimacy and connection are often met with divisive discourses. Taking a more nuanced perspective is important for both understanding consent and initiating meaningful conversation. Interestingly, this was the most sought-after room for bookings.

The Garden Room

Our impact on the environment and our planet has always been central to how we understand and deliver hospitality. As a business, we invested in an infrastructure aiming to reduce our carbon footprint, solar panels to power our premises, composting bins as an alternative to landfill, and active avoidance of single-use plastic. Instead, we required diners to bring in their own containers and take leftovers home. People would walk out of the Soup Bar with huge pots that they had brought in, to be seen later that night walking down the street carrying dinner for their households.

In the Garden Room, customers actively participated in replacing behaviours which negatively impact the planet with environmentally responsible alternatives.

We invited them to consider the small actions they could take to create a positive impact and drive change. While we may not have the ability to change the actions of multinational corporations, we firmly believe that in our own small ways, we *can* make significant changes through our behaviour.

Every evening in the garden, we organised quizzes on environmental and climate-related topics, discussing various strategies which can be implemented without much effort. The focus was on practical actions, where diners walked away armed with tools for immediate change.

These dining spaces were designed to evoke curiosity. We invited all our diners to re-engage their sense of openness and explore their individual contribution to creating a better world. Whether it was in the Garden Room, the Salon, the Kitchen, the Women's Room, or the Boudoir, our aim was to engage and gradually replace attitudes of prejudice with an open and inquisitive mindset.

'From little things, big things grow'—Paul Kelly and Kev Carmody.

MATTERS OF THE HEART

The Moroccan Soup Bar was never intended to be just a physical space, but rather a place of belonging that feels like home. Somewhere I could nurture my passionate desire to create a community in which the unconventional could be the norm.

I have born witness to a generation blossom with a great deal of pride.

All those who enter transcend from being customers to become a cherished part of our quirky family. Their stories are interwoven with my own, creating an atmosphere where love, empathy and understanding are on the menu each day.

The heart of the community beats with the joy of each milestone, every celebration; a wedding, a birthday, Iftar, Hannukah, Diwali, Lunar New Year, graduations, and wakes—the Moroccan Soup Bar is a personal affair.

My heart is full.

❋ ❋ ❋

The Soup Bar also changed my personal life in a way I did not anticipate. One night, amidst the bustling crowd of a café, my eyes were drawn to her. She exuded an irresistible charm and captivated me completely. Each glance between us made my heart flutter, as though it had found its rhythm for the first time, in perfect sync with hers. Her smile warmed the very core of my being, and her intelligence held a magnetic force that drew me closer. She introduced herself—it was an introduction I knew I would not soon forget.

At first, I resisted these feelings. I was not sure if my life was ready for something I knew to be so profound. Yet, despite my best efforts—despite the uncertainties that occupied my mind—they persisted.

Matters of the heart are stubborn, and mine had made its decision. She would become my life's partner. I chose her, and she chose me.

With her, I discovered life's beauty and a way of living that surpasses the confines of societal expectations and a connection that resonated deeply within my being. In the quiet moments of introspection, I grappled with these overwhelming emotions which tugged at my heartstrings. This marked the beginning of the next chapter in my life—one that has come to shape my understanding of love, relationships, and the delicate nature of human connection.

Never did I imagine such unwavering acceptance, mutual respect, support, and understanding. She fills me with a profound sense of joy and love that surpasses all other expectations. An extraordinary, unbreakable bond.

She is Alice.

SECRET
NO MORE

SECRET NO MORE

What are first memories? How do we locate time and place as children? I experience my memories like snippets. They are similar to the countdown at the beginning of a black-and-white movie, with flashes of events blurred by time and place, but when you pause on a certain event, everything crystallises and becomes clear.

My first memory took place in the late 1960s, Australia. I must have been four years old. I gather this through calculations and deductions—the birth of my youngest sister, who is four years younger than me.

My mother screaming, in so much pain, her screams shuddering through my little body as I panicked, not knowing what was happening. Someone yelled out, 'Call an ambulance!' as my eldest sister walked our mother towards the front door. It was there that she grunted and screamed in a voice that terrified me. I remember the fear; I could not make her pain stop. I did not have the words or the emotions to understand what was happening. My mother calling out for *her* mother to help her (who was in another country), then calling out to 'God ya Allah' to help her. Her water broke in the doorway. My sister announced that the baby was coming and that we couldn't wait for the ambulance. She told us to gather towels, blankets, anything soft.

My youngest sister came into the world in this way, on our doorstep. I watched my eldest sister deliver my youngest sister. Then the ambulance arrived and took them away. This is my first memory.

❁ ❁ ❁

Details of the ensuing events are too much to bear for a four-year-old child, or for the eleven years following. The scenes are too graphic, forever etched in my memory. I therefore made the decision not to share details of this horror so as not to re-traumatise the little girl within me. Instead, I searched for a metaphor to describe the gut-wrenching abuse of a child by a trusted family member.

In the midst of the panic and excitement of my little sister's arrival into the world, a predator lurked. His intentions hidden within our family's trust, he found an opportunity amidst the distractions of childbirth. He, a snake, patient, waited for the opportune time to strike. His venomous intent landed and wounded at the heart of innocence. He capitalised on the distractions of a baby's arrival, slipping through the cracks of excitement, panic, laughter, and celebration.

I was a child. I was four years old. With malicious and twisted intent, the predator stole my innocence, camouflaged by the very fabric that had enabled him: my family's trust. He observed a child's vulnerability, exploiting unguarded moments of adult distraction. He preyed upon my childhood, turning my innocence into trauma. A violation that defies words. A theft of the most sacred trust, a sense of security, and the essence of childhood. In that moment I was forever changed, as days formed into weeks and weeks turned into years.

I learnt the sound of the predator's footsteps, a unique thud heavier and more pronounced on the left side, with a slight untidy shuffle on the right. It seems ironic that for the person I most despised, I became so attentive to his every detail. Learning to unknow what I knew most has been my life's journey. I existed in this space alone, an aloneness which for many years would be my companion. A place where I guarded the innocence inside of me, a quiet place, where all motions slow.

I understand all-too well and recognise that the loss of innocence is too profound to be fully comprehended by words alone—it transcends the boundaries of language.

To convey the indescribable, I need to leave space for you, the reader. I invite you to engage your own understanding and to grapple with the gravity of these circumstances. To allow the space to contemplate the profound implications of sexual abuse. I write this in the hope that it emphasises the importance of *safeguarding children's innocence and creating a world where predators are barred from ever inhabiting such realms of being*.

I leave a blank page without description, as I care about the little me—and others—not to be re-violated.

What is it about society that enables violence and abuse to repeat? Is there a private school all abusers attend where they are trained in secrecy and manipulation? Perversity defines them, pre-empting every detail, covering their tracks, violating innocence.

But *why*? This question continues to defy comprehension.

The predator orchestrated a web in which he could move freely: charismatic, above suspicion, above reproach, giving him free access to me at will.

He was a socialite, well-connected and well-known, evading scrutiny.

He was a manipulator, who created dependencies; socially, financially, psychologically, and emotionally.

He reassured my mother that in his presence, we would all thrive, and she was fooled into believing his care was genuine. He rearranged the family's dynamic, crowning himself as head of the pack. He reduced my father's role to that of the nomadic loner and perfectionist panel beater, making sure he was either away or at work, while the predator took on all official affairs. He bought a shop, rented a house. He took possession of our family.

And just like that, the family's power was ceded.

This recurring violation lasted eleven years, from the age of four until I was fifteen years old. One day at school, I confided in a teacher (other than Helen), told her about the abuse. The school exposed the crime to my family.

Their response was to have me marry. And the cycle of violence and control continued, expressing itself differently and within different walls.

Until I woke up in hospital, and my life began.

The ramifications of my parents' decision to marry me off, when I was still a young girl and highly vulnerable, would be felt across my life. It would take years to come to terms with this secret reason for my early marriage. My parents' inability to deal with the actions of one male predator led me into the hands of another.

The community finding out about abuse within our family was too much for my parents to fathom or bear. It was easier to create what they thought was a solution.

As the years went by, it became more and more evident that dealing with the impacts of abuse and survival had taken a backseat. My emotions were repressed. I was living in survival mode. Deep down, a fundamental aspect of myself remained severed from my day-to-day existence— that of abuse.

Then, suddenly, the crisis hit. Seemingly without a warning, I entered a world of post-traumatic stress, repeated panic attacks, dissociation, and terrifying flashbacks. But somehow, I knew I would eventually be okay. At least my hope had not died.

Weakness defines the predator. Resilience defines me.

A message to all perpetrators: beware, *kids grow up*!

❀ ❀ ❀

It wasn't until I entered my thirties that I recognised the need for therapy, introspection, and healing. It is curious how the events of my childhood, the ones I endured as a young girl and teenager, seemed still so difficult to process as an adult. I found myself wondering … why is it that the impact of trauma intensifies with time? It is because, in retrospect, I realised that my entire life had been built on false assumptions, the destruction of innocence, and learned behaviours which should never have been learned?

One of my main struggles has been around my mother's knowledge. I have often wondered what she really knew about the abuse, and if I had been sacrificed.

I now appreciate that asking myself how much my mother knew is a privilege that was not afforded to her. Contemplating and posing this question from a place of adult safety does not provide me with any satisfactory answers to the questions I have asked myself for so many years.

VOICE
FOR OTHERS

Good evening, and welcome to the Moroccan Soup Bar.

Islam and Muslims have come under so much scrutiny and hostility, leaving no room for contemplation, and understanding of the intersectional issues impacting women.

No other topic has been more heavily debated than the status of women in Islam. People asking, 'Can women be empowered from within the Islamic faith?' And arguments that some interpretations of Islam have justified not only the subjugation of women, but also violence against women.

Patriarchy cuts across all societies and its expressions can be found throughout its culturally and religiously enshrined institutions.

A free and equal society is one in which we can shake off systems of oppression, bigotry and hate. In which the empowerment of all women is seen as a crucial step towards progress.

Once your mains are cleared, we will bring around mint tea and sweets.

SPEED DATE A MUSLIM

Our community engages people's inherent sense of decency. When given a chance, people are often wired for good. The year was 2015. ISIS-led terrorist attacks were wreaking havoc and terror across the globe. As the world changed around us and fear of Muslims turned to hate, Islamophobia took hold. Our staff and colleagues, Muslim women in particular, were acutely impacted. They became the subject of abuse in the streets by random passers-by.

While the external environment presented intense challenges, including a fear for their own safety, our staff remained gracious to our communities and diners.

It was obvious to me that the fear of others was

filling the gap left by the absence of our representation, shared spaces, and meaningful engagement. It was a time at which politicians positioned Islam in opposition to western values; helped by a media that thrived on sensationalist Islamophobia and populist storytelling, with our representation amplified only to perpetuate negative stereotypes. And as always, women bore the brunt.

Against this backdrop, I came up with Speed Date a Muslim.

The concept was simple: I wanted to remind people that we were not to be feared, that we were the neighbours, the friends, the colleagues with the same needs and aspirations as everyone else. It might sound naïve, yet everyday representation of us had almost disappeared. We needed to reclaim a space where we could be seen and our voice could be heard again.

Speed Date a Muslim would be a grassroots engagement initiative designed to break down stereotypes and build a rapport between Muslim women and those from other faiths or without religious beliefs. It would provide a safe space for people to engage, ask questions, share stories, and get to know Muslim women. It would be a way to promote respect, understanding, friendship, and learning in an informal, welcoming and relaxed setting. The aim was to reinforce education as the key to a functioning, respectful community. There was, of course, no romantic implication to this special speed-dating.

The rules for Speed Date a Muslim would be as follows: one hour for individuals from both groups of daters

(Muslim and non-Muslim) to interact, discuss, learn from each other, and connect. Importantly, no accusations nor judgements could be made. All themes of discussion had to be constructed as *questions* to the Muslim daters.

Then I needed to find the very brave and generous Muslim women who would agree to volunteer their time and make themselves vulnerable in order to embrace the exercise and build our community of daters. Their support was incredibly humbling, as I realised the trust these women placed in me, agreeing to be at the forefront of people's ignorance and curiosity. I guess my determination to ease the tensions in our society, and my belief in the decency and eagerness of people to learn about the Muslim daters sufficiently eased their minds.

And so, Speed Date a Muslim was born. It was a simple idea: a platform where conversations about Islam would be had from a woman's perspective. No longer would men be the sole interpreters of our faith; instead, together with these women, we would be the storytellers, the narrators of our own stories. There was no money involved—it was a free event, and no-one was paid. Complimentary tea and sweets would be served, and the reward was priceless.

❀ ❀ ❀

I advertised the event on social media and with printed flyers. The first Speed Date a Muslim event was scheduled for a Sunday afternoon after lunch service at our second venue, the Moroccan Delicacy. We arranged the tables and chairs, and the bench space in the hope that at least some people might attend. It was a sunny afternoon, so I had opened all the windows which wrapped around the restaurant. The symbol of *openness* was important, inviting even the most uncertain to feel welcome and comfortable.

It was almost 3pm. I had placed the freshly brewed pots of Moroccan mint tea and sweets onto each table, unsure of how many people would arrive, and particularly unsure of how many Muslim women would turn up. I assumed that in the worst-case scenario, our staff would engage one or two of the remaining diners in conversation.

A gentle breeze blew throughout the cafe, filled with the sweet scent of mint tea. My anticipation hovered in the air—*What if we get attacked*? But the what-ifs lingered for all of one minute, I looked up towards the doorway, the daters filed in: the first to arrive was a group of Muslim women, diverse in every sense. There were Australian Muslim women of various cultural backgrounds: Malaysia, Egypt, Somalia, Pakistan, Lebanon, Morocco, and Indonesia; some wore a hijab, of different shapes and forms, and some did not.

As more and more Muslim women arrived, they greeted each other. It seemed in one another they found *rahin*—a sense of belonging and safety—as they began exchanging stories as though they were long-lost friends. They were tender in their interactions, validating each other's realities. Their eyes filled with a sense of belonging which, to me, was a symbol of hope. They had come together not to be spoken for, but to reclaim their identities, to share their experiences, and to bridge the gap of understanding. This was the reason for their attendance.

Suddenly the restaurant was full. People kept coming until a line formed outside. I began by asking the only question I had organised: 'Are you a Muslim or a non-Muslim?' in order to place them in the appropriate seating arrangements. The restaurant was suddenly bursting at the seams, full to capacity; some people I had met before as diners and others who were first-timers.

I tapped a glass to get everyone's attention.

'Welcome to Speed Date a Muslim,' I announced.

I proceeded with the Acknowledgement to Country and clarified some basic rules for the event. I had only one requirement: that engagement needed to be respectful.

The first event was well received, with daters not shying away from respectfully getting to know each other.

The first question came from a man with an Akubra hat, directed to a woman wearing a niqab—a scene that seemed almost scripted: 'What are your thoughts about ISIS?'

She responded, 'ISIS are nothing to do with Islam and its values. Islam is a faith of peace, and there is no compulsion in religion. I am scared of ISIS and the way they represent my faith.' In that moment, I recalled being aware of my own internalised judgment of the niqab, and realised that I, too, needed to challenge some of my assumptions.

The hijab was a recurring theme for questions. It is often not seen as an expression of women's faith, but rather as a tool of her oppression. Questions such as, 'Who do you wear it around?', 'Why do you wear it?', 'Who makes you wear it?', and 'Are you about to get married?' inevitably circulate. In truth, the idea that a woman is 'choosing' to wear the hijab is so foreign. I am not inferring that the hijab is never forced upon women and girls. In fact, it is mandatory for women to cover themselves in some countries, including Afghanistan, Iran or Saudi Arabia. Men of every culture and faith will strive for control over women's bodies. However, in my experience, in Australia, the majority of Muslim women wear the hijab to visibly identify as Muslim.

At one Speed Date event, a man said, 'Quite frankly, I do not care for your jargon around the "hijibi hijabi"—whatever you want to call it. I don't find it sexy. I just want to see women at the beach wearing bikinis.'

I answered, 'In that case, why don't we also base laws and social codes around what *I* find sexy? Maybe a balding man is not my idea of sexy, and therefore balding should be illegal. That is the logical extension of your reasoning.'

A pause, as the man became very confused. 'What are you saying?'

I simply highlighted how judgemental his statement was and how he should consider its implication.

❁ ❁ ❁

On another occasion, someone asked, 'Well, what about answering the door without your hijab—is that weird for you?'

'No. It is just like you being naked and saying, "Hang on a moment, I'll put some clothes on."'

The rise of Islamophobia has made the very lives of Muslim women a commodity to be controlled. The hijab had become weaponised; women were to be rescued and liberated from it or be feared. It was really important to directly hear from the Muslim daters themselves about their personal motivations for wearing—or not wearing—the hijab: a symbol of their faith, their body, their choice.

Being a Muslim dater myself, I was often asked, 'What is Islam?'

I liked to respond by asking, 'What is Islam to *you*? What about it unsettles you and makes you fearful?' This simple questioning back opens an avenue for us to reframe the conversation, starting where people are at. One would not be expected to speak a language without having had the opportunity to learn it. Similarly, impacting change requires that the discussion is aligned with people's current understanding.

The bustling chatter in the room was punctuated by laughter, dispelling the weight of expectations and misconceptions. Daters had a great time, sharing questions and answers, seeking understanding, and most importantly connecting through their shared humanity. Despite the hostility they faced from the broader community, the Muslim women in attendance took on Speed Date a

Muslim almost like a duty; a calling to break the barriers of misunderstanding. These women gave up their time, every Sunday for many years, without fail. They stood at the forefront, greeting misconceptions and prejudices, and guided the conversation to build connections.

And all the non-Muslim people who came to Speed Date a Muslim left with a newfound understanding. The conversations they engaged in would change the way they saw Muslims, and Muslim women in particular. Speed Date a Muslim was not just an event at a restaurant. It is a testament to the people who came, to the power of conversation and storytelling, to people's empathy, and to the strength that lies in our unifying approach. It created a new way of combating Islamophobia, one conversation at a time.

The event became well-sought after. Not only did we host it inside our venues, we ran them across the state too: in rural towns, in schools, and in state-wide institutions such as the National Gallery of Victoria and the State Library of Victoria. This demonstrated people's appetite to hear an alternate version to the Muslim narrative than the one perpetuated by media and politicians.

As word spread about our initiative, we encountered a new kind of threat: not only were Muslim women in Melbourne being attacked for their perceived role in international terrorist attacks, we were now being attacked for our efforts in creating social harmony and peace. For one of our upcoming Speed Dates, we received a request from a Jewish group who shared the values of dialogue and bridge-building. We worked together to hold this initiative, centring it on the shared experiences of antisemitism and Islamophobia, particularly on women. Worryingly, this event also brought a new wave of threats. Far-right groups and individuals, threatened by the prospect of unity, sought to intimidate us, and undermine our initiative.

This included an increased number of hateful messages, filled with threats to rape, to harm, to kill. They made their intention clear on social media: they were rallying the troops and physically coming for us. The warning was obvious—'Cancel the event. If you go ahead, there will be consequences.'

The threats, while deeply unsettling, only reinforced the significance of our initiative. The women saw the opposition we faced as a testament to the importance of challenging hate and fostering understanding between communities.

The event would proceed. We were not going to be silenced by this toxic, racist, phobic mob. We immediately took measures to ensure the safety of all those who would attend.

With the added security, the event proceeded as planned. We engaged in thoughtful conversations, shared personal experiences, and dispelled many misconceptions. We emphasised the need for unity, solidarity, and support in combating discrimination faced by marginalised and targeted communities.

This event resonated deeply with the attendees, as they recognised the importance of standing together against all forms of bigotry. It became a symbol of resilience, unity, and hope, showcasing the potential of women in affecting positive change.

We are the change we dare to lead.

❖ ❖ ❖

With initiatives like Speed Date a Muslim, we challenged misconceptions and dismantled ignorance; fostered dialogue and helped heal our communities, using understanding and empathy as a bridge. Speed Date a Muslim was grounded in Islam's guiding compass, which points towards a path of compassion. It also enabled the support and empowerment of the Muslim women attendees.

We sought to identify the external factors, barriers, and tensions Muslim women navigate, as well as some of the internal tensions. Islam's foundational values of social justice, human rights, education, optimism, and truth-telling are far removed from the actual practices of many Islamic countries. We needed to navigate and contest public stereotypic representations while interrogating the implicit ways in which Muslim countries have conflated culture and tradition with Islam, rendering Islamic societies in dissonance with the very foundations and values of Islam.

In that regard, Speed Date a Muslim also became

an opportunity for Muslim women to become better acquainted with Islamic principles and able to distinguish those from cultural and societal expectations.

Although only just over three per cent of Australia's population is Muslim, you would be lucky to find an individual who, if you said the words 'Muslim' or 'Islam', wouldn't have a negative opinion. In fact, if I were not Muslim, and I believed in the accuracy of Muslim representation by media or politicians, I would also be fearful. Especially as there is no incentive to question what we think we know.

Often the *symbol* of that fear is women. It is not a Quran in a bookshop, or a prayer mat in a home, or a pilgrimage to Mecca—all tangible expressions of the declaration of faith and prayer. It is not the zakat—supporting the poor and the needy. Nor is it the fasting and breaking fast in Ramadan that are attacked. It is *women*.

So, for me, in advocating for women and for a better world where we can celebrate and respect our differences rather than fear them, I try to understand the perspectives of women from across the globe. When I look to other cultures, I always seek a woman's perspective.

I am of the view that there is a little bit too much testosterone in the world. It needs recalibration. Sometimes I'm asked, 'What does healthy masculinity look like?'

'An empowered woman,' I reply.

I believe that when we enable women, and when we make women's voices heard, we will progress society.

Over time, the important discussions taking place at

Speed Date a Muslim encouraged me to focus more on my own identity, which I further refined as I existed at the intersection of multiple identities, undoing the constraints imposed by social expectations while remaining true to my values as a Muslim.

Good evening, and welcome to the Moroccan Soup Bar.

Conversation salons have roots dating back to eighteenth-century France. Historically hosted by influential women known as salonnières, these gatherings brought together intellectuals, artists, poets, philosophers, and writers. Through the exchange of ideas, challenging traditional norms, and advancing knowledge, conversation salons played a significant role in shaping public opinion and influencing social change during the periods of enlightenment and revolution.

Tonight we are proudly hosting some of the most inspirational women to share their insights and inspire change.

The banquet will be brought out in courses throughout the evening. Please remember to leave room for dessert.

CONVERSATION SALON

Through the eyes of an innocent child; the salons of my childhood—'istiqbāl'—were where I felt safe and protected. As an adolescent, the salons became a place of navigating rituals and preparing for marriage. The salon was a formal space steeped in tradition, a silent witness to my evolution, and where I discovered the power embedded in the art of conversation.

The Conversation Salon emerged as a reinvention of the promises it held. This time the salon had become a vehicle for change, growth, and progress.

Hana in the middle, 1970s

Our Manifesto

This establishment operates
with a mindfulness
of the environment in
which we operate.
We are founded on principles
of social justice,
social equity and community engagement.
Open and diverse societies are foundational
to our expression.
We make every effort to be sustainable and
kind to the environment.

We hope you have a hunger for justice
and an appetite for the unconventional.

Expect the unexpected.

Welcome.

top: In full stride
left: Our manifesto
middle: Creating an appetite for
change
bottom right: The Garden Room

top: 'Women', installation by Sam Burke and Rebecca Umlaut, 2019
bottom: Women of the Moroccan Soup Bar

top: YES to dignity and respect
middle: Speed Date Victoria Police
bottom: The original four

All smiles, meeting Angela Davis (top) and amina wadud (bottom)

top: Freedom is a daily practice—a statement we live by
bottom left: Reunited with Helen
bottom right: The Salon

top and bottom: More extraordinary women of the Soup Bar

middle: Me and the speed daters

top: Feeling at home at the Moroccan Soup Bar

middle: Speed Date at the National Gallery of Victoria

bottom: The Conversation Salon

top: Meeting Camilla, HRH The Duchess of Cornwall

middle: One Plus One interview with Jane Hutcheon

bottom left: Melbourne Food and Wine, Local Hero

bottom right: Receiving my OAM from the Honourable Linda Dessau, AC CVO

top left: Farewelling the Moroccan Soup Bar
top right: Welcoming the sister Soup Bar, Two-Go
bottom left: The Boudoir
bottom right: The Women's Room

top: Feeding the healthcare workers

middle: The Kitchen

bottom: Cooking with a tagine

top: Me and Ai Weiwei at the Andy Warhol and Ai Weiwei exhibition, National Gallery of Victoria—I am a LEGO

bottom: Conversation Salon at the Women's Centre

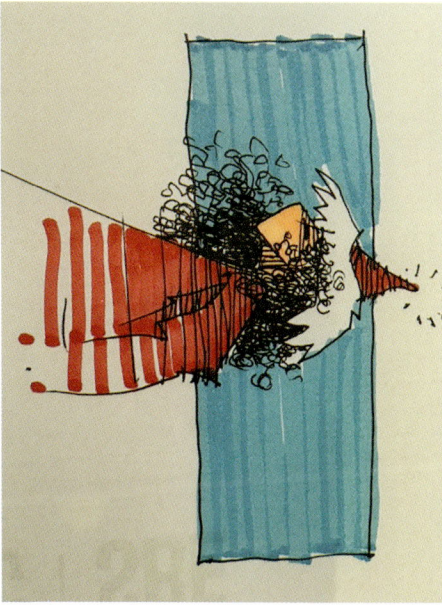

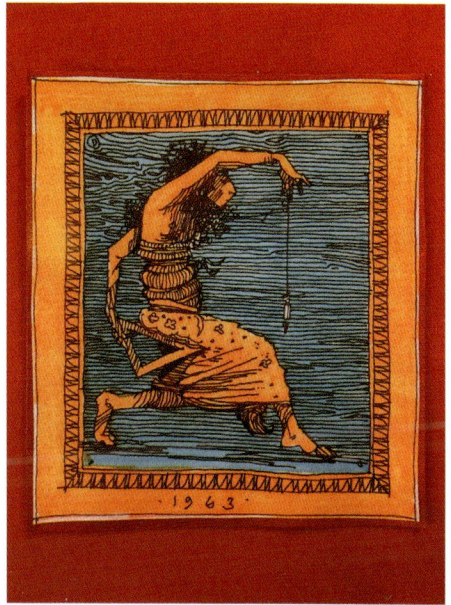

Portraits of me, by Mikko

top left: Friendship, Tracey and I
top right: Swimming in the cold winter waters of Melbourne's bay
bottom left: Sisters and nieces
bottom right: With my boys

Me and Alice

Dancing in the rain

2016. As the world continued to transform, social divisions crystallised through social media, and fewer safe platforms were available for meaningful conversations. Yet the problems of the world were intensifying ... climate change, economic inequality, refugee crises, political instability—and in Australia, the glaringly obvious need for reconciliation with our history and our continued oppression of the First Peoples.

The Conversation Salon followed our formula of open dialogue and respectful engagement, providing a safe space to hear and discuss the challenges we were facing, hear various perspectives, contest ideas, grow, and hopefully invite change from a grassroots level. We would showcase the voices of women—thinkers, artists, intellectuals, creatives, performers, and those who challenged convention.

Its format was a twist from the past. An evening banquet of food, offered up alongside a banquet of ideas, was held at the Moroccan Soup Bar in a dedicated room: the Salon. To emulate the atmosphere of Parisian salons of the eighteenth century, ours was illuminated with warmth, elegance, and sophistication. The room was decorated with plush red velvet drapes, sheer champagne curtains, and hand-etched brass Moroccan light fittings. On a wall, we had hand-painted Arabic calligraphy expressing a message of welcome. The centrepiece was a five-metre-long communal dining table made of reclaimed timber and specifically designed for this social gathering. Covering the floor was a large red Afghani rug. Chairs, poufs, and sofas were also part of the Moroccan collection. Music was curated to suit the theme of the night.

The run sheet, with its three presenters, was punctuated by food. Guests would be welcomed by our traditional mezze. We would gently guide them to sit, often alongside people they did not already know.

The first presenter would be introduced as the small warm tapas were being served. Our first guest would always feature the voices and perspectives of diverse First Nations women, including elders, activists, artists, academics and community leaders, united in their call for justice. There is no shortage of radical First Nation women. There is however a shortage of platforms to showcase them. Through their contributions, we discussed and learnt how to be better allies.

The main meal would accompany the second presenter, and then dessert and coffee would be served alongside the final speaker.

I MC'd each event, guiding the discussions, drawing out themes and ensuring key take-home messages. Those events were so much fun and so inspirational for all involved.

❋ ❋ ❋

Our first salon quickly booked out. The theme was 'Theatre of Narratives'.

It was followed by monthly events across various subjects reflective of current social tensions: 'Beyond Belly-Dancing, Bombs and Burqas', 'Climate Change and Changing Climate', 'Migration Movements and Moorings', 'Freedom of Speech: No Limits or Know Limits', and more.

The success was immediate and sustained. The appetite for what we were serving seemed insatiable. People craved meaningful engagement and self-reflection. We expanded, partnering with organisations who shared our values and further extending our reach and messaging. The Melbourne Immigration Museum hosted 'Building Cities on Colonised Lands' against the backdrop of a divided Australia and the Voice to Parliament Referendum. The National Gallery of Victoria hosted 'Arts and the Theatre of Narratives', and the Queen Victoria Women's Centre co-organised 'I Am Woman' on the contemporary issues impacting women.

❋ ❋ ❋

Some moments hold a special place in my heart, perhaps because they deeply shook me and gave me insight I was lacking. I remember the deep-stirred emotions upon hearing Mama Alto's performance of 'Over the Rainbow' following her discussion on the plight of transgender individuals. I also remember being moved to tears at hearing an anthem to the injustice faced by a mother by the young spoken-word poet, Zaynab Farah. The sheer power of Grace Vanillu's voice moved an entire room, calling us to action, to interrogate and challenge privilege and to learn to be better allies to First peoples.

Although I have only named a few, by no means does this diminish the contribution of all those who spoke at our Conversation Salons. They were all formidable women, carrying and delivering radical ideas, concepts, and calls to action. To all of them: thank you for your inspiration and your audacity.

❋ ❋ ❋

In 2017, we had the honour of hosting Angela Davis, an American activist and philosopher.

Growing up in an environment of implicit racism, I found my mentors in African American civil rights activists and other feminist writers: Audre Lorde, bell hooks, Arundhati Roy, and Gayatri Spivak to mention a few.

A powerful voice among them, Angela Davis was captivating. I connected with her words, which held me during times of extraordinary difficulty—especially when I found myself navigating the interplay of racism and misogyny.

As I became more active in public advocacy for marginalised women, one day the stars aligned. A mutual connection made the introduction and suggested I host

Angela Davis, who had travelled to Australia on another speaking initiative. And of course, without any hesitation, 'In conversation with Angela Davis' was organised.

Never did I imagine hosting *Angela Davis* in conversation. With delighted nervousness, I wanted everything to be perfect. I focused my charged energy into every minute detail, from the layout of the tables to the entire special banquet. I reimagined some old favourite recipes—the cauliflower stew on this occasion included lemon myrtle and was infused with Moroccan cumin and saffron. The combination of flavours danced on the palate. To honour women, I replaced the traditional baba ghanouj (which means 'father ghanouj') with a special mama ghanouj ('mother ghanouj') by refining and adding finely chopped, deseeded tomatoes, onion, fresh mint, and green capsicum—it was finger-licking yum!

I also made vegetarian kibbeh: cracked wheat, roasted capsicum, basil and pomegranate syrup, onion, preserved lemon chilli, olive oil, lemon, fresh mint—soaked, pounded, chopped, mixed—elevating the flavours to reflect the excitement I was feeling.

In anticipation of Angela Davis's arrival, I took meticulous care to ensure that everything was perfect. I swept and mopped the floors twice, wanting to honour the significance of her presence. I made sure the flower arrangements were imbued with symbolism; a harmonious blend of eucalyptus, olive branches, and modern orchids, as well as roses. I hoped she would notice, as it represented growth, peace, and diversity.

As the time drew closer for Angela Davis to arrive, I felt a mixture of excitement and nervousness swirling inside me. And then there she was, graceful, her presence towering over everyone else in the room. She was *tall*. She radiated wisdom, strength, and a profound sense of purpose. I was more than in awe.

As usual, I began with Acknowledgement to Country, and then nervously introduced Angela Davis. Her discourse that night is as important today as it was when I first read her work. Her perspective and contributions to women in particular was, and remain, revolutionary. Angela Davis has always been intersectional, and yet, as she explained, it took society decades to understand precisely what that concept meant. Her speech also veered into alliance with First Nations peoples, talking about the similarities between the experiences of African American and First Nations peoples.

As she spoke, I hung onto every word. Her voice was soft yet resonated deeply. It was as if the pages of her books had come alive and her ideas flowed freely into the room, inviting engagement. The connection I felt to her writings intensified, and in that moment, it was as though she was speaking directly to me. In fact, the whole audience probably felt the same.

We organised a panel discussion around racism, with speakers from Warriors of the Aboriginal Resistance (WAR), and from Australians for Native Title and Reconciliation (ANTAR), who presented the Australian experience of racism. We were invited to reflect on how a country that has not reconciled its history could move forward.

Angela Davis's enduring passion for justice, her determination to challenge societal norms, and her unrelenting commitment to equality was inspiring and validating. It was a reminder for me to keep agitating for change and to keep trust in the influence one person can have on another, even without knowing it.

I took down a quote from her that evening: 'I'm no longer accepting the things I cannot change. I'm changing the things I cannot accept'.

AFFIRMATION, RECOGNITION, FRIENDSHIP

One day, a filmmaker from the ABC came into the Moroccan Soup Bar. She said, 'This place is incredible. I've never seen anything like it.'

She introduced herself as Tracey, and went on, 'I would love to do a story about the Moroccan Soup Bar—your philosophy and the way this place works.'

Thus begun a conversation, quickly concluded by my response, 'Absolutely not.' There would be no public focus on the Moroccan Soup Bar. There would be no promotion, and definitely no media or story. I refused to draw attention to the women in crisis. Moreover, our ethos was built on the currency of word of mouth.

And yet I was tempted. After all, publicity could also shine a light on a successful working model that empowers women in crisis.

Despite my refusal, Tracey and I learnt to know each other. As a filmmaker, her interests lay in ethics, faith, and community-based stories. We quickly established trust. For all of her projects, she demonstrated professional integrity, ensuring the respect of the subject matter. Being Jewish, she understood too well the impact of stereotypes, and could relate the similarities of what was unfolding for Muslim women with the ever-present antisemitism. I knew, if anyone were to showcase the Moroccan Soup Bar, it should be her.

It was with this trust and rapport that I decided to go ahead one day, but it would take a few more years.

Sometime later, in 2016, at the height of Islamophobia— with increased attacks on women and, ironically, public spaces also becoming unsafe—Tracey discussed the proposal with me again. It had evolved. She now wanted to showcase Speed Date a Muslim, as she thought it was a simple yet effective initiative to combat prejudice and ignorance. She was particularly keen to highlight women's contributions in this space.

Regardless of my reservations, I knew it was time: our story needed to be told, adding our contributions to the fight against Islamophobia. I could work with Tracey to frame the conversation in a way that reflected us, so that we could advocate for Muslim women and offer a perspective that was not represented anywhere else in the media.

While I still had reservations, I also appreciated

the importance of this opportunity. Our society had profoundly changed—some of our staff were even being abused and threatened on their way to work. The environment was such that even some of our patrons felt the need to voice their opinion and share their unwanted views about Islam and Muslim women. Our environment had become unsafe.

I said yes. The proposal was accepted, our speed dating exercise would be featured in the ABC TV's Compass program, and suddenly rose to national exposure. The documentary was glorious! Joyful! Hopeful! It resonated with audiences across the country and spread our message far and wide.

Such media appearances generated greater public exposure, which meant increased interest and curiosity, but also increased hostility from those who did not appreciate our message. Dealing with increased racism, bigotry, and misogyny was a constant challenge.

After this, Tracey introduced me to ABC TV's One Plus One program, where I agreed to tell the story of my personal experiences growing up. This, too, was a daunting step. But it was also cathartic to give a public voice to my experience of violence and abuse.

When it comes to all matters of the media, I find myself calling Tracey for advice. Our relationship has grown into a deep friendship.

With increased attention came recognition. I was selected in 2015 to be a part of an art installation at the National Gallery of Victoria that included twenty

Australian activists who were not widely promoted and did not fit conventions, yet whose impact was no less profound than some well-known figures. This felt a bit surreal, and even more so because Ai Weiwei—the world-renowned artist—would be creating this installation.

His exhibit took the form of a grand room made from Lego pieces, each figure a two-metre-long portrait of the respective activists being portrayed and accompanied by a quote of their choosing. Mine was, 'I strive to rectify the imbalance where women in all societies and religions are among the most vulnerable and marginalised.'

I accidentally grew into this public persona. I was quite content in the familiar walls of the Moroccan Soup Bar and considered myself lucky and privileged to be working alongside such amazing and resilient women. And yet, I felt simultaneously drawn out of the Moroccan Soup Bar and saw value in contributing to all these social engagements. I gradually stepped into my public role, where I now advise on a myriad of social and topical issues.

Public speaking never came easy, and at times still doesn't. I recall the first event, engulfed by emotions before I step onto the stage. My nerves turned my entire body into jelly. I became that little girl again, facing a sea of people with eyes fixated on me. Fear crept in—what if my words faltered, what if I lost my ability to speak altogether? The inner voice of that little girl resurfaced, now embodied in me, as an adult figure standing in front of this audience. I wondered if anyone could see what was happening within me.

I summoned every ounce of courage to calm these anxieties and began to speak.

Stepping onto larger public speaking platforms introduced new fears. Now, I step up I hold my own hand, and imagine I am speaking for that little girl.

❀ ❀ ❀

I found myself in places I never imagined I'd be in. In 2018 I was invited to speak at the Women of The World Conference for International Women's Day, held in London. It felt surreal, that I was going to the UK to meet Camilla, the Duchess of Cornwall (now Queen of England), who was the Conference's patron. *What am I supposed to wear? I am comfortable in trousers and I'm not about to present as anyone other than myself!* A reception had been organised at Clarence House, and centred solely around the contributions and rights of women and girls.

Camilla's address demonstrated a commitment to the empowerment of women and girls. She challenged institutions, talked about the reality of subjugation, violence, and systems of inequality for women and girls. I wished the settings would have allowed to engage her in a conversation about the history of Australia, but it just wasn't possible.

After the speeches, some of us were invited to meet her. I was neither excited nor intimidated, though I found the whole etiquette bizarre. We were given a crash course in proper decorum, including how to curtsy.

Yeah, right! I thought to myself. I couldn't curtsy if my life depended on it.

When it was my turn to approach, I clasped Camilla's hand in both of mine, shook it, and said, 'Hello, I am Hana, how are you?', hoping that would suffice.

We talked and it turned out that she was genuinely curious about the impact of Islamophobia on women and about the Speed Date a Muslim initiative. In essence, we just had our very own speed date session.

❈   ❈   ❈

The Moroccan Soup Bar is a place where lives have been transformed and accomplishments celebrated. We have received numerous awards and industry recognition. These acknowledgements reaffirmed our commitment in ethical hospitality, reinventing and pushing the boundaries of what dinning could be.

When I was notified of my nomination for an Order of Australia Medal (OAM), all sorts of emotions surged within me. On the one hand, I felt a deep sense of elation, validation, and achievement. It was an undeniable affirmation of our hard work and commitment to women's rights. On the other hand, I felt an unmistakable reservation; aware that the very system behind this award was itself founded on a legacy of colonialism and racism acutely impacting First Nations communities. Meeting Camilla and talking about empowerment of women in her country was one thing, but accepting this award was much more confronting. It became a paradox. How could I accept an award from a system that perpetuated inequality and marginalisation?

For me, recognition of this nature is built on the silent struggles and resilience of countless women from diverse backgrounds relegated to the margins—their contributions undervalued or erased. Accepting an award like the OAM comes with responsibility: it requires committing to honour those who have been excluded, amplifying the voices of those who society deliberately ignores, and challenge the status quo.

It was with this realisation, and this responsibility, that I reconciled my acceptance of the OAM.

I would use this platform to further amplify marginalised voices, to challenge systemic racism and advocate for change. I hung the medal in the restaurant for all staff and diners to see and celebrate—it was also theirs.

❋ ❋ ❋

We stand on the shoulders of extraordinary women and celebrate those who have pushed societal boundaries—those who dared to dance when they were told to sit still.

Conformity rarely gives birth to innovation or progress. The real magic happens when we embrace those who do not uphold conventions, who dare to speak up.

For me, the importance of having a voice has been shaped by many experiences—it did not come easily. Being loud was never just a choice for me; it was a necessity. *Giving* voice—shedding a light on racism, sexism, trauma, and the interplay of systems of oppression—has become my life's purpose. I am compelled to challenge injustices (and un-truths). For me, it is a matter of survival.

❋ ❋ ❋

Throughout our twenty-five years of running the Moroccan Soup Bar, colleagues have become friends, and friends have become family. We support each other and mentor one another, guiding the newcomers, forming true sisterhood, and reinforcing respect.

Perhaps the most meaningful recognition is had in a quiet sense of pride. A validation of the community's role as a nurturing ground for leaders who carry forward values of compassion and kindness. A legacy we built together extends far beyond the walls of Fitzroy North. As I see the young now leading in their respective fields, lawyers, doctors, artists, and more, I am filled with pride that our shared values will continue to shape a more compassionate and just world.

PANDEMIC

March 2020. COVID 19 arrived.

Despite all the alarms raised by medical professionals and scientists worldwide, it seemed to come as a surprise to our politicians. 'Without warning', the virus stopped everything and everyone. We became fixed in time, forced to navigate an incredibly tragic and dangerous situation within a complex set of social parameters.

We entered the pandemic in a profoundly unequal society: inequalities in employment, security, housing, finances, access to information, and access to healthcare to name a few. And importantly, our various communities entered the pandemic with different levels of trust in our Government.

As a whole, Australians have a high trust in their national Government, yet this sentiment is not shared by all. Institutional distrust is generally associated with feelings of powerlessness, and the belief that the institutions do not represent nor act in the interests of the people they are supposed to serve. In the context of the last twenty years of increased xenophobia and fear of the other, it is not a surprise that many marginal groups tend to be suspicious of Government intentions and messaging. For those who were already marginalised, already disengaged at the onset of the pandemic, this suspicion was amplified. As a consequence, because there was no clear, trusted Government messaging, it became inevitable that the information that *did* reach these communities did not come from trustworthy sources. This created a huge problem for the effective delivery of public health.

As for my personal experience, I remember precisely Thursday the 12th of March 2020; the day I realised the world was about to take on a new trajectory. Together with my staff, we were preparing our departure to Colac—country Victoria—for the following morning, where we were catering for an International Women's Day event and for which I was also the keynote speaker.

I was following the news of course, watching the stream of information on these infections, spreading like wildfire. Australia's isolation from the rest of the world gave us more time. Yet watching the catastrophe unfolding around the world, from China, Iran, to Italy, told us the obvious: this was coming here, and we needed to ready ourselves in the little time we had left. For me, this meant making sure my family was safe. Home was easily dealt with. Alice, a scientist, had transformed our home into a physical containment room—nothing (and no-one) would come in without being thoroughly sprayed with disinfectant. Never had I absorbed so much ethanol in my life.

It of course also meant the Moroccan Soup Bar staff had to be safe. And importantly, we needed to keep our wider community safe. For my staff, safety had always come first. It was in fact the very reason for their employment at the Moroccan Soup Bar. It seemed so different now, as all signs indicated they would be safer at *home* than coming to work.

For the patrons, the situation was equally confronting: the very formula that enabled us to thrive—snaking queues, congested dining rooms, communal dining— was not compatible with an emerging respiratory virus landscape.

Every thought I had suggested that our very success had become a threat to the women we strove to support, and to our diners. In parallel, our Government was signalling that all would be okay.

On the following morning, we drove to Colac, prepared the room, the catering—the event went well. Yet I had been preoccupied the entire day with this sense of responsibility and of uncertainty about what action to take. What must I do to keep people safe, in this terrible unknown that was making its way toward us? I decided, it had to be precaution: we would pause until we could have a better understanding of the situation. This was the only decision that felt appropriate. This is how I decided the temporary closure of the Moroccan Soup Bar. By doing so, we would keep our staff and patrons safe. We announced our decision the following day, Saturday the 14th of March 2020.

The original Moroccan Soup Bar—183 St Georges Road—sadly, never reopened.

Our Government was trying to grapple with the enormity of the event and its disconnect from various communities was becoming evident. As a result, official information and guidance on the situation failed to reach many, in particular individuals of non-English speaking background. Our staff was no exception. Many mistrusted the Government's intentions, and most did not have access to reliable sources of information. So, we used the early days of our pause to provide this most needed information. It was delivered directly from experts, scientists willing to also contribute their part in making our society a little safer. In the room, I and others would translate.

On one occasion, about forty women, staff and relatives, all at safe distance from each other, were talked through how a respiratory virus could be transmitted. They were provided with the opportunity to raise questions about the unfolding situation. And there were many. In fact, we came to realise that many people did not know the difference between a virus and bacteria, their modes of transmission—without even that fundamental understanding, how could we expect anyone to comply with lockdown and isolation rules if they did not understand their rationale?

Not long after, our country entered its first lockdown, and awaited this first 'wave'. The mood was grim yet an incredible sense of humanity, of solidarity spread around the nation. Many could not work anymore, and others—in particular in the healthcare sector—were under incredible pressure. The health of the country was in their hands. It was obvious to me that we needed to help. And we would do so by providing what we do best: hospitality.

We would deliver healthy meals to the healthcare workers of various hospitals around Melbourne during this first lockdown. This was our way to show our gratitude, appreciation, and support those who were putting their health at risk to protect all of us. In order to sustain the action, we established a pay forward campaign, whereby someone would pay for a meal that would then be delivered to a healthcare worker. Over Zoom meetings, we rallied like-minded friends and colleagues from different industries—communication, philanthropy, advertising (after all, most had lost their work routine)— and organised the internet campaign.

The logistics at the Moroccan Soup Bar were well-oiled. It seemed we had been training for this moment—we were efficient! Our kitchen transformed into a surgeon's theatre practice: only essential staff, masked and gloved, at a safe distance from each other were allowed in. The anteroom (the room between the kitchen and the outside) had become a decontamination zone: everything and everyone would follow a rigorous 'sterilisation' procedure. And finally, the front of the shop was transformed into the distribution chain: it was there that we would add sweet treats and write personal notes of gratitude and thanks to accompany their meals. And we would deliver our hundreds of healthy nutritious individual lunch packs to hospitals daily across Melbourne. We hoped they would feel our support and that these meals would at least bring them a sense of normality in this chaos. The food was amazing. I heard from one of the nurses that sometimes the smell of the Moroccan Soup Bar meal awaiting them was the highlight of their day!

The community of individuals around us was formidable and sustained the initiative for the entire first lockdown—five weeks, four hospitals.

As the pandemic and successive lockdowns became our new normal, through the Moroccan Soup Bar we continued to play our role in ensuring accurate information could reach our communities. This included information on vaccination, even transforming our premises into a vaccination hub and offering a side of the chickpea bake in place of the regular sweet treat.

By the time the Melbourne lockdowns eventually ended we had fully moved to our other Fitzroy North premises, 500 metres down the road.

❀ ❀ ❀

The attitude with which I navigated COVID was one of absolute acceptance of the science, and the values of optimism and compassion.

The original Moroccan Soup Bar, as we knew it, had ended. I knew, deep down—without any foreseeable hope of opening for dine-ins, coupled with landlords trying to secure income in a market that felt unpredictable and insecure—I would have to forfeit the property. I did not even have time to grieve. It was time for evolution and something new.

In the scheme of things, even after twenty-five years, it did not matter. When something is finished, it's finished. You can struggle to reach this acceptance, or you can try and make sense of the world around it. I'd had plenty of training in how to behave in adversity.

I emptied the premises to hand back to the landlord. Physically dismantling the bar and taking things apart. It was both therapeutic and cathartic. The once-bustling Marrakech souk of Melbourne's Fitzroy North had now transformed into a space for my internal contemplation. With every dismantling of physical furniture, my deep emotions came pouring out. I found myself just speaking to the wall; the tangerine wall I had painted with my father all those years ago. I talked to the wall about the secrets and stories we had witnessed over the years, and in doing so realised I was closing the Moroccan Soup Bar in much the same way I opened it: on my own.

I asked the wall if it remembered my late father, *Allah Yerhamou*—a man of paradoxes. He was an absent guardian in my early years, yet his presence and support were evident during the establishment of the Moroccan Soup Bar. Never judging me, even when I embarked on ventures he did not understand. He was of his time; a true artisan, he refused to use electric tools, crafting cabinets and benches with time-consuming labour and precision. His hands could mould and shape the most intricate details. He taught me the art of mixing paints; he helped me transform the empty 'FOR LEASE' space into the birth of the Moroccan Soup Bar. In his quiet wisdom, he did not only restore physical surfaces, he silently expressed his commitment to my own restoration and healing.

Through building, painting, and carpentry, he conveyed a love that surpassed words. His painting was a silent apology. In crafting the cabinets and benches my father built a healing bridge between us—a testament to his character and enduring love. This time my father stood beside me. It felt like redemption for him. His actions conveyed the unspoken apologies for the lost years and the protection I was denied.

The emptiness of the Moroccan Soup Bar mirrored my now-stripped bare emotions. Reflecting on poignant moments, my thoughts then turned to my mother, and how I yearned for a different conversation.

Towards the end of her life, my mother succumbed to a debilitating illness. Motor neurone disease. The news was gut-wrenching for our family. Mum was anxious by nature, she found comfort amongst her family at home. I went back to the familiar role of carer. We transformed her bedroom into a hospital and we committed ourselves to a roster, ensuring she was never alone and had around-the-clock care in the presence of her family.

I was devastated. Regressing to the role of the child, desperately seeking a cure for the incurable. Nothing else mattered.

Soon after her diagnosis, she took me aside and, as was her habit when she had a secret to share, she clasped my hands in hers with a purposeful look, conveying the sadness of a lifetime.

'Hana, please forgive me,' she said.

In that moment, I was confused. I protested, 'For what? There's nothing to forgive, you are the best, Mum!'

I just wanted her to feel well, oblivious to the full significance of her words.

I have come to understand that forgiveness is not a singular act but a process, an evolution of understanding and acceptance. However, not all actions are worthy of forgiveness, nor should they be. In understanding the profound impact of sexual abuse, I have carved out a space for my wellbeing; one that stands firm in its refusal to forgive the unforgivable.

My mother did her best, and though it was not enough, I understand. Her reasons were often beyond her control. As a child, I lacked the capacity for comprehension—I only existed with the desperate need to feel safe and protected.

Many years passed and wounds have softened.

Embracing the love of a mother and her inadequacies in protecting her daughter.

I wish I could just tell you, Mum, not as a protest against your sense of guilt. I wish I could take your hands in mine, snuggle into your embrace.

I love you, Mum. I forgive you, Mum.

Allah yerhamek. Rest in peace.

❈ ❈ ❈

Overwhelmed by emotion, tears sprang to my eyes. *The end of an era.*

I farewelled my moment in this Moroccan Soup Bar. The stories. The legacy. The growth. The energy in that space, that room, held us. Literally. I accepted that our time was finished here and said goodbye.

TRANSFORMATION

Following the shock of the pandemic, the Moroccan Soup Bar concept survived and evolved. We left our sister venue to eventually relocate to North Melbourne.

Our last evening service in Fitzroy North was emotional. It was a bittersweet farewell. As the restaurant filled, every inch resonated; a collective gesture of love and gratitude. In that final moment we were a united community. Speeches spontaneously erupted, more than just words; it was ceremonial. I 'tapped the glass' to make an announcement …

My voice quivered, filled with sadness. I faltered. Customers completed my sentences, a reassuring echo …

Good evening, and welcome to the Moroccan Soup Bar.

In life, we cross paths with individuals who, in the face of unimaginable atrocities, exhibit remarkable acts of kindness and maintain their inherent goodness. These individuals exist everywhere, inspiring hope and connection. They highlight the enduring bonds that unite us in our shared humanity. It is with extraordinary gratitude, admiration, and respect that I recognise these amazing individuals who have touched my life, who managed to preserve their humanity and mine. Their willingness to act with compassion and kindness counteracts the abominable acts and uplifts us all.

The connections we forge with people who embody unwavering kindness, even in the face of adversity, are a living testament to the enduring bonds which transcend our differences. Our shared experiences solidify our resilience, reminding us that together we can be the change we want to see in the world, even in our darkest times. I have been a proud witness of a generation that has blossomed.

We hope you enjoyed our final dinner service. Goodbye Fitzroy North. Thank you for the privilege.

The following day, we held a garage sale, where the artefacts collected over the years were bought and found new homes. Each item held a piece of our history, and the community eagerly competed to take these memories with them. Stories once housed within our walls were now scattered across Melbourne—on someone's desk and bookshelf, in a lounge room, in a kitchen, in a garden. In an instant everything was gone, marking the beginning of the metamorphosis. I kept one lamp that I had bought in Morocco as a reminder of the Moroccan Soup Bar, the Souk of Fitzroy North.

The space, now empty, stood as a silent testimony to the Fitzroy North community. The legacy lived on, not just within those physical artefacts but in the hearts and minds of those who had been part of this our extraordinary journey.

In the quiet aftermath, as the last traces of the community's presence disappeared, the realisation settled: while the physical space may be elsewhere, the spirit of Fitzroy North lingered in the lives and endeavours of those who had called it home.

In 2022, the business moved location to North Melbourne and changed the means through which we deliver both food and messages. We concentrate on catering, hosting functions and events, and a small in-house dining area. This new reality allows us to continue to empower women and reach people in their private locations, where they can still enjoy our hospitality and warmth.

The Moroccan Soup Bar started out by supporting women and engaging with our broader community. It has now also become a trusted voice for women's rights, social justice, and the practical application of important social justice causes.

As I reflect on the quirkiness of our hospitality style, I remember the hypothetical scenario posed to me during my career in women's services: 'A woman with two kids calls you from a phone box with nowhere else to go. What do you tell her?'

I will tell her to come inside and pull up a seat.

HEALING

RECKONING

Back in 1993. I lived alone in a small flat—the space mirrored my independence, the freedom I had found in leaving my married life behind, completing a second year of studies, and working in the women's refuge sector.

I was self-reliant; a sense of wellbeing had settled upon me. I had re-established a relationship with my sons. The wounds, although still present, were no longer at the forefront of my mind. I had learnt to live with them to better my life.

One day, everything seemed eerily at peace. I was at work, sitting in front of a client for a counselling session. It began like any other. I was listening intently, reflecting back, validating the client's experience. She sat before me, her voice trembling with pain, as she began to share the harrowing details of her abuse. Her words cut through me like shards of glass. As she continued and unveiled the depths of her trauma, an overwhelming sensation surged within me; a panic I could not comprehend. This space was meant for her healing—I worried for her, and her needs, as I felt my attention begin to fracture. I now know her story was a trigger I had not anticipated, disrupting our session and my composure.

A rush of nausea consumed me, forcing me to abruptly leave the room.

I became confused, could not gather my thoughts, my head was spinning, I started questioning my sanity. Then, I felt my lungs compress, incapable of catching air. I thought I was having a heart attack. I was overcome by sheer terror. I stumbled, desperately seeking relief from the inner turmoil. In that moment, a close colleague intervened and calmed me. She took over the client's counselling session, ensuring she was okay. Then she sat with me, explaining she recognised the tell-tale signs of a trigger and panic attack. She gently guided me to seek the help of Dr Helen D (another Helen!). She specialised in early childhood trauma therapy.

❁ ❁ ❁

I entered Helen's office for the first time. A wave of uncertainty came over me. My heart raced and my palms were sweaty. I was flooded with doubts and questions—how could this person truly comprehend the depth of my struggles? Could I trust her with these fragments of my thoughts and emotions? With my innermost vulnerability? I tried to delve into the conflicting emotions within me, my desire for help wrestling against my fear of judgment.

Helen's office felt more like a home than a psych clinic, capturing the essence of warmth and safety: a couch sitting opposite a child's play table, scattered with shapes and toys and coloured pencils. At once, I was comforted, relieved not to be confronted by a clinical setting.

As Helen opened the door, she radiated a soothing aura. In a gentle tone of voice, she said, 'Hello, Hana.'

It was with Helen, in that space, that I felt safe, and my true healing began.

The uncertainty in my voice was palpable as I cautiously shared glimpses of my story, testing the waters of trust. Each word carried the weight of my vulnerability, as I yearned for acceptance and understanding.

Therapy sessions with Helen marked a new chapter in my life's journey: an exploration of the deep wounds that had laid dormant beneath the surface, needing recognition. It would be a long process before I would truly heal. After all, I was twenty-eight years old. My life had been marked by sexual abuse, domestic violence, and forced separations from my children, and yet I had never dealt with the impact. I did not realise I would ever need to confront these traumas. In fact, with today's hindsight, I know this young Hana had not yet integrated that these abuses had happened, nor had she reconciled that they created immense trauma.

Looking back, I realise I was surviving day to day. Therapy gave me the ability to live and become whole. There, I explored and understood the cause and impact of abuse and realised that this dissociation had become necessary for my survival.

Though the process was not easy—at times, I felt as though I was completely paralysed, unable to move past the anxiety that overwhelmed and constrained me—therapy gave me a path to healing. Over the years, Helen's support and guidance helped me discover a path of understanding and unravelling the complexities of my childhood and marriage traumas. She helped me realise the strength in seeking support and the transformative power of healing. She chaperoned my emergence from the shadows of the past which had, at times, consumed me. She became my most trusted person.

For this, I owe a debt of gratitude to Helen, who gave me back to myself.

❀　❀　❀

Sexual violence and abuse are perverse acts of deprivation and control. Victims of these crimes are stripped of their sense of self and confidence and internalise the ensuing shame and humiliation. The healing process requires an unlearning of that shame, moving from survival to self-discovery. I needed to truly face my internalised sense of shame, self-hate, humiliation and self-loathing, as difficult as this was. Indeed, by shedding these feelings that were not mine to bear, I accepted that none of the abuse was my fault.

As I peeled away these layers, which I had carried throughout my life, I embraced self-care as a radical form of self-love, where my wellbeing mattered. Healing led me to confront my perpetrators, thereby shifting the responsibility where it rightfully belonged.

Finding my voice in the silence of pain required acceptance: the audacity to speak my truth, to be free from the weight of expectations placed on me from a young age. Speaking out was not just an act of defiance against my abusers; it was an expression of my right to exist without fear. A reclaiming of my own sense of self that had been stripped away.

Transformative healing required that I turned my focus inwards, with self-care through reading, listening to music, meditation, yoga, art. These aspects of my existence were neglected for far too long.

An important aspect of my healing has taken place in my relationship to music. Music was, at many times in my life, forbidden and always an escape. I have always found that music possesses a profound ability to touch my soul. In moments of despair, music has been soothing;

dissolving the aches of longing I felt within. Through music, I found the means to express the emotions which words often failed to capture.

Oum Kalthoum was unparalleled until I found myself captivated by the soul-stirring melodies of Sinéad O'Connor. The first time I heard her, her voice hung in the air. I was captivated. I sat in silence for a long time, allowing the lyrics and melody to wash over me. At the time I did not realise that Sinead was dealing with her own battles of abuse. Her voice was so compelling—a call to justice—and it reverberated profoundly.

Tina Turner's music was another revelation. In her songs, I felt an electric surge pass through me, as if she had ignited a fire within my very being.

Tori Amos's haunting voice enveloped me. It was as if her words were speaking directly to my soul, each word unravelling a layer of emotions I had long kept hidden. Her ability to transform pain into art was breathtaking.

A common thread uniting these three amazing women artists was their unwavering devotion to rejecting society's subjugation and channelling their trauma through music. Their songs conveyed life's hardships through their music, voices, and lyrics of protest. In certain ways, elements of their journeys mirrored my own. Their music was my companion. As I faced my own struggles, I often turned to these women's songs for guidance and solace.

While writing this book, I heard of the devastating passing of Sinéad O'Connor.

The magnitude of her death, to me, revealed a

surprising level of attachment. Her art transcended the boundaries of personal connection, touching the hearts and souls of those of us who have survived. I feel I have shared a part of my life with her without her knowing me. Thank you for the music, Sinéad.

During this difficult period of healing, I also needed to reconcile my identity as a Muslim woman. I had questions that endured since I was a young girl. I decided to study Islam further, in particular its history, philosophy, and relationship to women. I came across prominent Muslim women thinkers. Their writings and contributions evolved into a movement of gendered justice within Islam. Among others, I read amina wadud—a scholar challenging gender expressions within Islam. With these writings, I reconciled my rightful place in Islam, a place too long denied by customs and traditions.

I have come to appreciate that healing from trauma is a process that takes many forms and happens in various stages throughout life. Though therapy was instrumental, integrating its learnings and beginning a journey of self-care and healing was equally essential.

Embracing a sense of entitlement, to fully heal, investing in time, with myself and on myself. I now sometimes find my voice and expression in painting. It is where I lose track of time. In this tranquil space, serene and calm, art rejuvenates me.

Now, many years older, as I listen to the music of Oum Kalthoum, I no longer seek answers. Instead, I experience a sense of nostalgia in the timeless voice, a sweet melancholy. In her epic songs my memories intertwine, soulful, dissolving the boundaries of time to connect 'young Hana' to the woman I have become. To the struggles of my mother, and to the liberating journey to becoming free. As I listen, I am transported into a place where healing and time coalesce.

❈ ❈ ❈

My resilience is drawn from the many women in my life. I am in absolute gratitude to them, my teachers, therapists, sisters, friends, partners, and work colleagues.

In these women I found a nurturing space, safe to explore my vulnerabilities, reassuring me that I was not alone. I discovered the power of vulnerability and the ability to revisit layers of my unresolved past trauma. They listened, loved, and supported me, never judging or dismissing my pain. These women became my inspiration, light, and hope, guiding me through some of the most difficult of moments. They comforted and validated me.

This story, while located in place and time, is not unique. The constant search for autonomy and freedom is in every woman.

THE SEA

As I conclude these chapters, I take a break and go for a swim in Melbourne's Port Philip Bay. A soothing ritual that has endured since the pandemic. In the depth of the sea … Swimming—long forbidden by my family, yet so vital and natural.

Could it be that they knew the independence, liberation, and freedom the sea offers?

I have always been drawn to the sea. Although I never learned to swim, I felt attracted by its vast majesty. Standing on its shores, I escaped the trauma of abuse, momentarily. The sea is where I shed the weight of my troubles, and my imagination is unhindered.

For a time, my family and I lived in Mentone, a Melbourne seaside suburb. Our house was directly across the road from the beach, and I was always cautious of the water's depths. Despite my fear, I found comfort at the water's edge. Each day, the sun set over the water, leaving behind a sinking feeling. I feared the day's abandonment over the horizon, giving way to a darkness in whose shadows abuse was free to roam. I wished I could, as if by magic follow the daylight into its horizon.

The sea bore witness to the unspeakable pain I endured. From the safety of the shores, its waters offered me visual comfort, allowed me to share my pain.

The 'seawater' was blamed for the first act of violence in my marriage, and yet it was my emotional escape, my respite, carrying my troubles into the unknown distance. How I longed to swim, denied the ability by the constraints of past circumstances.

Trust did not come easily. Survival instincts guarded my vulnerability. When Alice entered my life, she created an environment where I could safely explore my deepest insecurities and fears. Alice, a swimmer, despite my repertoire of well-crafted excuses, knew.

She guided me into the pool and taught me to swim— in chlorinated pools and warm beaches. One kilometre a day became my routine, a place of rejuvenation. In swimming, I found a healing ritual, like food, a nourishing daily necessity.

As the world grappled with the challenges of the pandemic, and societies locked down, swimming pools were closed. Public pools, private pools, rivers, lakes—I couldn't even find a puddle! I was longing for the feeling of being submerged. It was during this time we discovered open-water swimming in the chilly waters of Melbourne's winter. South Melbourne beach beckoned, 4.8 kilometres away from our home. We were permitted to travel 5 kilometres.

This quickly became a cherished ritual, keeping me and a community of swimmers afloat during testing times. Open-water swimming surpassed the impact of the pandemic and now forms a delightful part of my much-loved routine.

Few experiences compare to the liberating sensory experience of open-water swimming. In the vast majesty I immerse myself seamlessly, weightless in the water's embrace. The noise and worries of the world fade, replaced by the sound of my breathing, and the quietness of the waters beneath. With each stroke, I glide through the soothing waves, feeling myself called to venture further. Each breath draws me closer, I keep swimming, I am *free*.

One and a half kilometres, I reach the sweet spot, I am in the sea's most serene embrace.

The seawater is sweet indeed.

EPILOGUE

In these pages I have written of when I was a child surrounded by war.

As my story comes to its conclusion, it is impossible not to acknowledge the brutal reality of wars that are unfolding around the world. The main casualties are innocent civilians, overwhelmingly women and children.

I am someone who has a lot of say, and yet I am unable to find words.

My wish is for enduring justice and peace. Our world, and our children, deserve no less.

ACKNOWLEDGEMENTS

In writing my story, I am filled with profound gratitude. Alice, you made this book possible. Tracey, thank you for your unwavering support, friendship, encouragement, guidance, and the laughter.

To the Melbourne Books team—David, for his support in everything involved in the publishing of this book; and Sophie, Ellen, and Georgia, for all their commitment.

Helen, your meticulous attention to every detail, your encouragement in moments of doubt.

Dean and Jacqui, from Minter Ellison, your goodwill has helped this story be told.

Daniel, with gratitude, for your artistry, your visual eye. Thank you for the front cover.

My sons—I love you.

My sisters and brother—thank you for your love and support. I am grateful for the bonds we share.

My nieces—I'm so proud of you.

To Leanne, with a deep sense of gratitude, your constant love and support during the inception of the Moroccan Soup Bar, and particularly the earlier years when my boys came back. Thank you.

Women of the Soup Bar: thank you for the privilege, you are the heart of the Moroccan Soup Bar.

Customers, thank you for your support over the last twenty-five years.

Elisa Grassa, thank you for your support in the early days of setting up the Moroccan Delicacy.

A huge thanks to the awesome speed daters.

To everyone who, amidst their own busy lives, offered a helping hand, a kind word, or a moment of compassion— your impact is infused into these pages.

To those who do not conform, to those who find they do not belong; you are my inspiration.

This acknowledgement is a sincere expression of gratitude to all of you who contributed, in ways big and small, to enabling this story to be told.

Thank you.

WOMEN'S HELPLINES

Centre Against Sexual Assault (CASA)
1800 806 292

Djirra
1800 105 303

Elizabeth Morgan House Aboriginal Women's Service
03 9482 5744

inTouch Multicultural Centre Against Family Violence
1800 755 988

1800 RESPECT
1800 737 732

Women's Information and Referral Exchange (WIRE)
1300 134 130

BupBup Wilam Aboriginal Child and Family Centre
03 8459 4900

Australian Muslim Women's Centre for Human Rights
03 9481 3000

Multicultural Centre for Women's Health
1800 656 421

Lifeline
131114, SMS 0477 13 11 14

Safe Steps Family Violence Response Centre
1800 015 188

Immigrant Women's Health Service
(02) 9726 4044 or (02) 9726 1016